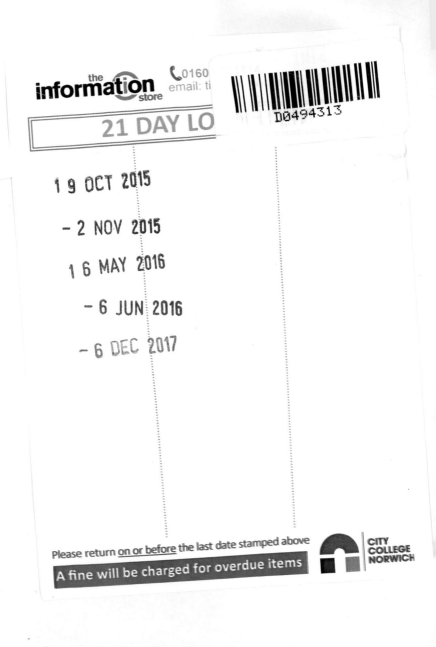

the information store 📞0160
email: ti

D0494313

21 DAY LO

1 9 OCT 2015

− 2 NOV 2015

1 6 MAY 2016

− 6 JUN 2016

− 6 DEC 2017

244 938

The RSC Shakespeare

Edited by Jonathan Bate and Eric Rasmussen
Chief Associate Editors: Héloïse Sénéchal and Jan Sewell
Associate Editors: Trey Jansen, Eleanor Lowe, Lucy Munro, Dee Anna Phares

TWELFTH NIGHT

Textual editing: Eric Rasmussen
Introduction and Shakespeare's Career in the Theatre: Jonathan Bate
Commentary: Eleanor Lowe and Héloïse Sénéchal
Scene-by-Scene Analysis: Esme Miskimmin
In Performance: Karin Brown (RSC stagings) and Jan Sewell (overview)
The Director's Cut (interviews by Jonathan Bate and Kevin Wright):
Sam Mendes, Declan Donnellan and Neil Bartlett

The RSC Shakespeare

WILLIAM SHAKESPEARE

TWELFTH NIGHT

Edited by
Jonathan Bate and Eric Rasmussen

Introduced by Jonathan Bate

Macmillan

Published 2010 by
MACMILLAN PUBLISHERS LTD
registered in England, company number 785998, of Houndmills, Basingstoke, Hampshire RG21 6XS.
Companies and representatives throughout the world

ISBN-13 978-0-230-24384-2 paperback

10   9   8   7   6   5   4   3   2   1
19   18   17   16   15   14   13   12   11   10

Printed in China

CONTENTS

INTRODUCTION

'HOW HAVE YOU MADE DIVISION OF YOURSELF?'

'What is love?' asks Feste the clown in one of his songs. It is a very old question. One of the most influential answers to it comes from ancient Greece in the imaginary voice of the comic dramatist Aristophanes in Plato's dialogue called the *Symposium*. Love, says Aristophanes, is a quest, a journey in search of our lost other half.

The idea is explained by way of a story about human origins. Originally there were not two sexes but three – male, female and a mixture of the two called androgynous. Furthermore, the original humans were round, with four hands, four feet and two faces. Humankind then began to have presumptuous ambitions. We rose up against the Olympian gods. Zeus therefore decided to weaken us by cutting us in two, 'like an apple halved for pickling'. So now we have two legs, two arms, one face and the sensation that we are only half ourselves. We yearn and wander, hoping that one day we will find the other half that is literally our soul-mate. If the original whole of which you are a half was male, your desire will be for another male (as seems to be the case with Antonio in this play – and Orsino when he falls for 'Cesario'?); if female, another female (Olivia desiring the disguised Viola?). These two orientations are what we now call homosexual.

Only if your original was androgynous will you be drawn to the opposite sex, as Viola is to Orsino – and Sir Toby, who has the play's largest role, to Maria. When one of us meets his or her other half, 'the actual half of himself', then, the *Symposium* explains, 'the pair are lost in an amazement of love and friendship and intimacy, and one will not wish to be out of the other's sight even for a moment: these are the people who pass their whole lives together, and yet they could not explain what they desire of one another'.

A myth of this kind is a piece of storytelling that answers to a profound and enduring human belief: that we are somehow incomplete without love, without a partner. And that in an ideal world we would all have exactly the right partner. We know viscerally that desire and reproduction are forever bound to conjunction and splitting: two people join as one in the act of love; we are made out of a mixture of X and Y chromosomes, of male seed and female egg, of two distinct genetic lines.

If love is a quest for an idealized version of our own selves, it is easy to understand our fascination with twins. They seem to be the living embodiment of the single self split in two; the extreme case of conjoined twins vividly conjures up the *Symposium*'s tale of the original human as an unhalved apple. At the same time, a certain anxiety has always been attached to the phenomenon of twins. In ancient Greece it was assumed that a woman who bore twins must have been impregnated by two different men. Some mythical twins represent idealized unity – as with Castor and Pollux, the 'gemini' or heavenly twins who symbolize perfect friendship – but others represent opposition or splitting. A nymph in Ovid's *Metamorphoses* has twins fathered by Apollo, god of music and light, and Mercury, god of theft and shady dealings; a pair of girl twins in Edmund Spenser's epic romance of Shakespeare's time, *The Faerie Queene*, respectively embody chastity and eroticism; in another of Ovid's poems, the *Fasti*, a girl called Lara is raped by Mercury and bears the Lares Compitales, who become guardians of the crossroads. These twins become symbolic of how the story of our lives is made of a perpetual sequence of choices, as alternative ways open before us.

Perhaps the most potent of all narratives about twins are those in which a brother and sister are separated soon after birth, meet when they are grown up and fall passionately and unashamedly in love with each other: Siegmund and Sieglinde, as portrayed in Richard Wagner's *Die Walküre*, might be considered western culture's highest exemplar of the motif. Brother–sister incest was sometimes explored in the Renaissance theatre – most notably in John Ford's darkly brilliant *'Tis Pity She's a Whore* – but Shakespeare steered away from this dangerous matter. His way of recreating the *Symposium*'s originary androgyne was by cross-dressing Viola as 'Cesario', the lovely boy-actor with whom both man and woman, both Orsino and Olivia, fall in love. Puns on 'woman's part' and 'small pipe' (meaning both voice and male sexual organ) leave no doubt that alluring androgyny is implied here:

> For they shall yet belie thy happy years,
> That say thou art a man: Diana's lip
> Is not more smooth and rubious, thy small pipe
> Is as the maiden's organ, shrill and sound,
> And all is semblative a woman's part.

William and Ann Shakespeare's twins, Judith and Hamnet (alternatively spelled Hamlet), were born in February 1585. Their father's fascination with the dramatic possibilities of double selves is apparent from his early *Comedy of Errors*, where he adapted a classical story about separated male twins and mistaken identity, but complicated it by giving the brothers servants who are also identical twins. Then in the summer of 1596, the eleven-year-old Hamnet died. Shakespeare had lost his only son and Judith would be forever bereft of her second self. Though we should always be wary of inferring authorial autobiography from the words of fictional characters in a play, there is an inescapable poignancy to the images of loss in *Twelfth Night*: when Feste sings of sad cypress ('Come away, death') or Viola alludes to a funeral monument, it is tempting to think of Shakespeare's own lost boy. Olivia mourns a brother, while Viola assumes that hers has been drowned. When she takes a male disguise and 'becomes' Cesario, it is as if she impersonates her own opposite-sex twin: 'I am all the daughters of my father's house, / And all the brothers too.' She herself explains that the lost Sebastian is the model for her performance of male behaviour ('For him I imitate').

The principal source of *Twelfth Night*'s tale of siblings lost and found, and of a cross-dressed servant sent to woo on behalf of a master whom she loves herself, was a novella by Barnaby Riche called 'Apolonius and Silla'. There the brother and sister who are the originals for Viola and Sebastian are not twins but 'the one of them was so like the other in countenance and favour that there was no man able to discern the one from the other by their faces, saving by their apparel, the one being a man, the other a woman'. Critics sometimes express puzzlement that Shakespeare makes so much of the resemblance between Viola and Sebastian, given his presumed personal knowledge that boy–girl twins are not identical. In modern terminology, it is generally accepted that monozygotic fertilization is always same sex (in fact, recent research has shown that in certain rare cases of genetic abnormality it is possible to have boy–girl monozygotic twins). But Riche's original premise reveals the absurdity of this criticism of the plot: siblings don't even have to be twins to look remarkably alike.

One of the greatest challenges for a writer is to imagine what it would be like to be a member of the opposite sex. The particular demand faced by Shakespeare and the boy-actors who played his women's parts was to get beyond the age's conventions of proper female behaviour, which commended silence and submissiveness. 'Cesario' is partly a device to give Viola an active voice, to enable her to break the shackles of passivity. But the lovely combination of quick-witted facility, wonder and vulnerability with which she slots into her impersonation is something more than a reaction to social convention or codes of propriety. In terms of the play's imaginary world, Viola plays Cesario so effectively because of her prior knowledge and love of Sebastian – this is what allows the otherwise implausible conceit of Olivia's marrying Sebastian in the belief that he is Cesario. In terms of the play's creative origin, it is tempting to speculate that the germ was sown by Shakespeare's observation of the intuitive understanding between his twins as they learned to speak and to play together.

Shakespearean comedy often imagines a journey from the secure womb of the family to a world of shipwreck and isolation, and thence to the bond of marriage. The characters lose themselves to find themselves. Broken families are restored in the same instant that new families are anticipated through the pronouncement of love-vows. The climax of *Twelfth Night* is one of the great reunion scenes, as the parted twins are joined:

> ORSINO One face, one voice, one habit, and two persons,
> A natural perspective, that is and is not!
> . . .
> ANTONIO How have you made division of yourself?
> An apple cleft in two is not more twin
> Than these two creatures. . . .

The language is richly suggestive of one made two and two made one, of the cleft apple from the *Symposium*'s myth of origins, and of the workings of nature combined with the trick of art (a 'perspective' was a distorting glass that created the optical illusion of one picture appearing as two). In a single action, brother and sister find both each other and their object of desire.

And yet. The peculiar poignancy of *Twelfth Night* comes from the sense that there are many losses even in this moment of wonder. Antonio, who has been like a brother and even a lover to Sebastian, is left alone. Malvolio has been humiliated just a little too far. The union of Sir Toby and Maria leaves Sir Andrew isolated – he was adored once, too, but we cannot imagine that he will be again. And Feste is there to sing another sad song of time and change. Above all, Cesario is no more: Orsino closes the dialogue by addressing Viola by her boy-name onc final time before she assumes her female garb and becomes his 'fancy's queen'. But 'fancy's queen' is the very language of that shallow courtly love with which Orsino had tried to woo Olivia: the language that Cesario cast off when he/she began speaking in his/her own voice. In the closing moments of the play, Viola does seem to revert to the silence and passivity of orthodox female behaviour.

What is going through her imaginary heart at this moment? Even as Sebastian and Orsino are found, Cesario is lost. Could Viola be saying goodbye to the feigned twin into which she has made herself?

The name 'Cesario' suggests untimely birth – as in 'Caesarean section', a baby 'from his mother's womb / Untimely ripped'

(*Macbeth*, Act 5 scene 7) – but the character undergoes an untimely death. A few months before starting the comedy of *Twelfth Night*, Shakespeare completed his deeply meditated tragedy of *Hamlet*. There are unfathomable cross-currents at work here: in creating and destroying Cesario, perhaps Shakespeare too is saying a goodbye. To his own Hamnet. Viola is diminished when bereaved of her invented second self. Was this Shakespeare's delayed response to poor Judith's desolation on the loss of her twin?

In preparing to direct the play for the Royal Shakespeare Company in 2009, Gregory Doran, himself a twin, noticed a coincidence neglected by nearly all the legion of Shakespeare's biographers and critics. Hamnet and Judith Shakespeare were baptized on 2 February, the feast of Candlemas (which celebrates the presentation of the baby Jesus in the Temple in Jerusalem – a fitting moment for the baptism of a treasured first son). And it was on the that very same festival day seventeen years later, 2 February, Candlemas, that *Twelfth Night* was performed (the earliest perfor- mance of which we have a record) before the law students of the Middle Temple in 1602. Malvolio describes Cesario/Viola as 'Not yet old enough for a man, nor young enough for a boy. As a squash is before 'tis a peascod, or a codling when 'tis almost an apple: 'tis with him in standing water, between boy and man'. On 2 February 1602, Judith was in standing water between girl and woman. By turning Viola into Cesario and allowing Sebastian to return from the devouring sea of death, Shakespeare allowed himself the consoling fantasy of a seventeenth birthday reunion for his own separated twins.

THE FOUNTAIN OF SELF-LOVE

A more immediate occasion for the play's meditations on love and identity seems to have been Shakespeare's friendly rivalry with Ben Jonson. Shakespeare had been writing courtship comedies for many years when Jonson came onto the theatrical scene at the end of the 1590s with a more hard-edged satirical vein of drama that tapped into the psychology of 'humours' – the idea that aberrant behaviour (which is readily comic and worthy of satire) could be attributed to an excess of a particular passion or obsession or to temperamental imbalance (too much choler or melancholy). Jonson seems to have fallen out with Shakespeare's acting company early in the new century. At this time he wrote a play called *The Fountain of Self-Love, or Cynthia's Revels* for the Children of Her Majesty's Chapel, the 'boy-actors' company that, to judge from a famous piece of dialogue in *Hamlet*, was perceived by Shakespeare and his fellows as something of a threat to their own prestige. Jonson's double title was innovative and not a little pretentious: Shakespeare may well have been mocking it with *Twelfth Night, or What You Will* (his only double title). In pricking the bubble of inflated language, as he habitually does, Feste may be glancing at Jonson's verbosity. 'I might say "element", but the word is over-worn': 'element' is a key word in Jonson's humoral lexicon. And again, in response to Antonio's 'I prithee vent thy folly somewhere else', Feste says 'Vent my folly! He has heard that word of some great man and now applies it to a fool. Vent my folly!' Since *The Fountain of Self-Love* contains such phrases as 'vent thy passion' and 'vent the Etna of his fires', 'some great man' might almost be Jonson.

The fountain in Jonson's play is that of Narcissus, who drowned while trying to kiss his own reflection. Shakespeare's Illyria is also a place of self-love. Yellow-stockinged Malvolio in particular is a Narcissus figure, but there is also a certain vanity about Orsino as he plays the role of the courtly lover. Viola, by contrast, is the opposite of a self-lover. She comes back from drowning and speaks in the voice of the desiring woman whom Narcissus neglected:

> Make me a willow cabin at your gate,
> And call upon my soul within the house,
> Write loyal cantons of contemnèd love
> And sing them loud even in the dead of night,
> Hallow your name to the reverberate hills
> And make the babbling gossip of the air
> Cry out 'Olivia!' O, you should not rest
> Between the elements of air and earth,
> But you should pity me!

As intimated by the 'reverberate hills' and the echo effect '"Olivia!"
O', the 'babbling gossip of the air' alludes to the mythological figure
of Echo, who pined away as a result of her unrequited love for
Narcissus.

Jonsonian comedy is peopled by narcissists. *Twelfth Night*
responds with an astonishing exploration of the relationship
between knowledge of self and sympathy for others – which we
might call 'echoing' – in the composition of human identity. 'I am
not what I am'; 'Be that thou know'st thou art'; 'I swear I am not
that I play'; 'Ourselves we do not owe'; 'Nothing that is so is so'; 'You
shall from this time be / Your master's mistress'. These paradoxes
and promises are the word-music of Illyria that 'gives a very echo to
the seat / Where love is throned'.

MASTER-MISTRESS

The play begins with what sounds very like a fifteen-line unrhymed
sonnet, spoken in the voice of an archetypal Renaissance lover, an
aficionado of the great Italian poet Petrarch's sonnets in praise of his
lovely but unobtainable Laura. This kind of love thrives on
unrequitedness. The poet-lover uses imagery of music and the sea,
of food, of rising and falling. Such language is typical of the vogue for
sonneteering in the 1590s: every self-respecting Elizabethan poet
had a sheaf of sonnets to his or her name. Like the conventional
sonneteers, Orsino alludes to figures from classical mythology, in his
case Ovid's Actaeon hunted down by the dogs of his own desire for
lovely but chaste Diana. When Olivia appears, Orsino says that
'heaven walks on earth', which is just what an orthodox sonneteer
would say. He revels in the 'sovereign cruelty' of his stony lady, as all
Petrarchan lovers do.

But he is then thrown by the beauty of a lovely boy. The
audience, however, knows that Cesario is really Viola, a girl in
disguise, and that the body parts so lovingly blazoned by Orsino
really are the 'woman's part' – except they are not, since (at least the

majority of) the audience also knows that Viola is a part written for a boy-actor. 'Thou dost speak masterly' says Orsino in response to Cesario's eloquence. In so doing, he allows himself to become the master mastered by the servingman. Or rather the boy. Or is that the girl? Or the boy-actor?

Orsino claims that a woman's love is of less value than a man's because it is driven solely by 'appetite', which may be sated, whereas his capacity for desire is infinite:

> There is no woman's sides
> Can bide the beating of so strong a passion
> As love doth give my heart, no woman's heart
> So big, to hold so much. They lack retention.
> Alas, their love may be called appetite,
> No motion of the liver, but the palate,
> That suffer surfeit, cloyment and revolt.
> But mine is all as hungry as the sea,
> And can digest as much. . . .

Here he again resembles a sonneteer, whose love is limitless because it is defined by being unrequited. And when he reappears at the end of the play, Orsino duly speaks another of his fifteen-line sonnets, this one ending with the most hackneyed rhyme in the sonneteer's repertoire:

> Why should I not, had I the heart to do it,
> Like to th'Egyptian thief at point of death,
> Kill what I love? — a savage jealousy
> That sometimes savours nobly. But hear me this:
> Since you to non-regardance cast my faith,
> And that I partly know the instrument
> That screws me from my true place in your favour,
> Live you the marble-breasted tyrant still.
> But this your minion, whom I know you love,
> And whom, by heaven I swear, I tender dearly,
> Him will I tear out of that cruel eye,
> Where he sits crownèd in his master's spite.
> Come, boy, with me. My thoughts are ripe in mischief:
> I'll sacrifice the lamb that I do love,
> To spite a raven's heart within a dove.

But then he discovers that Cesario is really Viola and he is able to resolve the tension – which is also the tension of Shakespeare's sonnets – between love for a lovely boy and desire for a woman:

> Your master quits you. And for your service done him,
> So much against the mettle of your sex,
> So far beneath your soft and tender breeding,
> And since you called me master for so long,
> Here is my hand. You shall from this time be
> Your master's mistress.

If Orsino is the conventional Elizabethan sonneteer, Olivia is parodist of the genre. The sonneteer customarily enumerates his lady's beautiful body parts, one by one in that device known as the 'blazon'. Olivia enumerates her own: 'I will give out divers schedules of my beauty. It shall be inventoried, and every particle and utensil labelled to my will: as, *item*, two lips, indifferent red: *item*, two grey eyes, with lids to them: *item*, one neck, one chin and so forth.' But then love – for Cesario – catches up on her and she finds herself deploying the blazon in all seriousness: 'Thy tongue, thy face, thy limbs, actions and spirit, / Do give thee five-fold blazon'. She begins to wish that 'the master were the man' – or the man her master. Viola, meanwhile, gains a voice by becoming Cesario. In the sonnet form, the object of desire is just that, an object. In *Twelfth Night*, Viola, desired by both man and woman, is a feeling subject. Vulnerable, and thus forced to become an actor ('I am not that I play'), she soon finds herself in the situation of desiring the man she has been sent to persuade to love someone else – an analogous twist to that of Shakespeare's sonnets, which begin with the speaker persuading the fair youth to marry, then dissolve into the speaker's own love for the youth.

Sonnet 20 startlingly begins 'A woman's face with Nature's own hand painted / Hast thou, the master-mistress of my passion'. There is only one other phrase in the literature of the age that may be readily compared with the coinage 'master-mistress': Orsino's 'Your master's mistress'. Perhaps as good an answer as any to the hoary old question of the identity of the lovely youth to whom the bulk of Shakespeare's sonnets are addressed is 'a figure who resembles Cesario'.

Twelfth Night is an extraordinary exploration of the permutations of desire or, to use the terminology of an Elizabethan admirer of Shakespeare called Francis Meres, of 'the perplexities of love'. Both Orsino and Olivia love Viola in her disguise as Cesario. Viola loves, and wins, Orsino, while Olivia has to settle for Sebastian. Orsino insists on continuing to call Viola Cesario even after he knows that she is a woman. Sebastian is puzzled, though grateful, to find himself whisked to the altar by the wealthy and beautiful Olivia, but he cannot have had time to fall in love with her. The person who really loves him is Antonio, who reminds him that for three months, 'No interim, not a minute's vacancy, / Both day and night did we keep company'. He follows his beloved despite the risk to his own life: 'But, come what may, I do adore thee so, / That danger shall seem sport, and I will go'. Like a sonneteer, he speaks of being spurred on by his 'desire, / More sharp than filèd steel' and, again, of paying 'devotion' to 'his image, which methought did promise / Most venerable worth'. He is rewarded for his devotion by being left alone and melancholy, again in the exact manner of a sonneteer turned away by his frosty mistress. It is very easy to imagine Antonio going away at the end of Twelfth Night and writing something on the following lines, addressed to Sebastian:

> They that have power to hurt and will do none,
> That do not do the thing they most do show,
> Who, moving others, are themselves as stone,
> Unmovèd, cold, and to temptation slow:
> They rightly do inherit heaven's graces
> And husband nature's riches from expense.
> They are the lords and owners of their faces,
> Others but stewards of their excellence.

This is actually the speaker of Shakespeare's sonnets (in Sonnet 94) as he finds himself rejected by the fair youth or the lovely boy. In so many of the plays it is Shakespeare's chilly, self-controlled young men – Prince Hal in Henry IV, Angelo in Measure for Measure, Bertram in All's Well that Ends Well – who take, who are the lords and owners of their faces. His open-hearted women – Rosalind in

As You Like It, Innogen in *Cymbeline*, Viola above all – are never like this. They *do* do the things they most do show. They move others but they are never stone themselves, unless men turn them to coldness. His women give – of their selves, their wit and their courage. And that is why his women's parts, even though written for boys, have been great gifts to actresses down the ages.

ABOUT THE TEXT

Shakespeare endures through history. He illuminates later times as well as his own. He helps us to understand the human condition. But he cannot do this without a good text of the plays. Without editions there would be no Shakespeare. That is why every twenty years or so throughout the last three centuries there has been a major new edition of his complete works. One aspect of editing is the process of keeping the texts up to date – modernizing the spelling, punctuation and typography (though not, of course, the actual words), providing explanatory notes in the light of changing educational practices (a generation ago, most of Shakespeare's classical and Biblical allusions could be assumed to be generally understood, but now they can't).

Because Shakespeare did not personally oversee the publication of his plays, with some plays there are major editorial difficulties. Decisions have to be made as to the relative authority of the early printed editions, the pocket format 'quartos' published in Shakespeare's lifetime and the elaborately produced 'First Folio' text of 1623, the original 'Complete Works' prepared for the press after his death by Shakespeare's fellow-actors, the people who knew the plays better than anyone else. *Twelfth Night*, however, exists only in a Folio text that is exceptionally well printed. It is one of the few Shakespeare plays where there is hardly any textual difficulty or controversy.

The following notes highlight various aspects of the editorial process and indicate conventions used in the text of this edition:

Lists of Parts are supplied in the First Folio for only six plays, not including *Twelfth Night*, so the list here is editorially supplied. Capitals indicate that part of the name which is used for speech headings in the script (thus 'SIR TOBY Belch, Olivia's kinsman').

Locations are provided by the Folio for only two plays, of which *Twelfth Night* is not one. Eighteenth-century editors, working in an age of elaborately realistic stage sets, were the first to provide detailed locations ('*another part of the town*'). Given that Shakespeare wrote for a bare stage and often an imprecise sense of place, we have relegated locations to the explanatory notes at the foot of the page, where they are given at the beginning of each scene where the imaginary location is different from the one before. In the case of *Twelfth Night*, the entire action is set in Illyria, on the eastern Adriatic coast, and moves principally between the households of Duke Orsino and Countess Olivia.

Act and Scene Divisions were provided in the Folio in a much more thoroughgoing way than in the Quartos. Sometimes, however, they were erroneous or omitted; corrections and additions supplied by editorial tradition are indicated by square brackets. Five-act division is based on a classical model, and act breaks provided the opportunity to replace the candles in the indoor Blackfriars playhouse which the King's Men used after 1608, but Shakespeare did not necessarily think in terms of a five-part structure of dramatic composition. The Folio convention is that a scene ends when the stage is empty. Nowadays, partly under the influence of film, we tend to consider a scene to be a dramatic unit that ends with either a change of imaginary location or a significant passage of time within the narrative. Shakespeare's fluidity of composition accords well with this convention, so in addition to act and scene numbers we provide a *running scene* count in the right margin at the beginning of each new scene, in the typeface used for editorial directions. Where there is a scene break caused by a momentary bare stage, but the location does not change and extra time does not pass, we use the convention *running scene continues*. There is inevitably a degree of editorial judgment in making such calls, but the system is very valuable in suggesting the pace of the plays.

Speakers' Names are often inconsistent in Folio. We have regularized speech headings, but retained an element of deliberate inconsistency in entry directions, in order to give the flavour of Folio.

Thus FESTE is always so-called in his speech headings, but is generally '*Clown*' in entry directions.

Verse is indicated by lines that do not run to the right margin and by capitalization of each line. The Folio printers sometimes set verse as prose, and vice versa (either out of misunderstanding or for reasons of space). We have silently corrected in such cases, although in some instances there is ambiguity, in which case we have leaned towards the preservation of Folio layout. Folio sometimes uses contraction ('turnd' rather than 'turned') to indicate whether or not the final '-ed' of a past participle is sounded, an area where there is variation for the sake of the five-beat iambic pentameter rhythm. We use the convention of a grave accent to indicate sounding (thus 'turnèd' would be two syllables), but would urge actors not to overstress. In cases where one speaker ends with a verse half-line and the next begins with the other half of the pentameter, editors since the late eighteenth century have indented the second line. We have abandoned this convention, since the Folio does not use it, and nor did actors' cues in the Shakespearean theatre. An exception is made when the second speaker actively interrupts or completes the first speaker's sentence.

Spelling is modernized, but older forms are very occasionally maintained where necessary for rhythm or aural effect.

Punctuation in Shakespeare's time was as much rhetorical as grammatical. 'Colon' was originally a term for a unit of thought in an argument. The semi-colon was a new unit of punctuation (some of the Quartos lack them altogether). We have modernized punctuation throughout, but have given more weight to Folio punctuation than many editors, since, though not Shakespearean, it reflects the usage of his period. In particular, we have used the colon far more than many editors: it is exceptionally useful as a way of indicating how many Shakespearean speeches unfold clause by clause in a developing argument that gives the illusion of enacting the process of thinking in the moment. We have also kept in mind the origin of punctuation in classical times as a way of assisting the actor and orator: the comma suggests the briefest of pauses for breath, the colon a middling one and a full stop or period a longer pause. Semi-colons, by contrast, belong to an era of punctuation that was only just coming in during Shakespeare's time and that is coming to an end now: we have accordingly only used them where they occur in our copy-texts (and not always then). Dashes are sometimes used for parenthetical interjections where the Folio has brackets. They are also used for interruptions and changes in train of thought. Where a change of addressee occurs within a speech, we have used a dash preceded by a full stop (or occasionally another form of punctuation). Often the identity of the respective addressees is obvious from the context. When it is not, this has been indicated in a marginal stage direction.

Entrances and Exits are fairly thorough in Folio, which has accordingly been followed as faithfully as possible. Where characters are omitted or corrections are necessary, this is indicated by square brackets (e.g. '[*and Attendants*]'). *Exit* is sometimes silently normalized to *Exeunt* and *Manet* anglicized to 'remains'. We trust Folio positioning of entrances and exits to a greater degree than most editors.

Editorial Stage Directions such as stage business, asides, indications of addressee and of characters' position on the gallery stage are only used sparingly in Folio. Other editions mingle directions of this kind with original Folio and Quarto directions, sometimes marking them by means of square brackets. We have sought to distinguish what could be described as *directorial* interventions of this kind from Folio-style directions (either original or supplied) by placing them in the right margin in a different typeface. There is a degree of subjectivity about which directions are of which kind, but the procedure is intended as a reminder to the reader and the actor that Shakespearean stage directions are often dependent upon editorial inference alone and are not set in stone. We also depart from editorial tradition in sometimes admitting uncertainty and thus printing permissive stage-directions, such as an *Aside?* (often a line may be equally effective as an aside or a direct address – it is for each production or reading to make its own decision) or a *may exit* or a piece of business placed between arrows to indicate that it may occur at various different moments within a scene.

Line Numbers in the left margin are editorial, for reference and to key the explanatory and textual notes.

Explanatory Notes at the foot of each page explain allusions and gloss obsolete and difficult words, confusing phraseology, occasional major textual cruces, and so on. Particular attention is given to non-standard usage, bawdy innuendo and technical terms (e.g. legal and military language). Where more than one sense is given, commas indicate shades of related meaning, slashes alternative or double meanings.

Textual Notes at the end of the play indicate major departures from the Folio. They take the following form: the reading of our text is given in bold and its source given after an equals sign, with 'Q' indicating a Quarto reading, 'F2' a reading that derives from the Second Folio of 1632, 'F3' from the Third Folio of 1663 and 'Ed' that it derives from the subsequent editorial tradition. The rejected Folio ('F') reading is then given. Thus, for example, '**2.3.25 leman** = Ed. F = Lemon' means that at Act 2 scene 3 line 25, the phrase 'I sent thee sixpence for thy Lemon' clearly made little sense and a later editor has concluded that a compositor's (or possibly scribal) error occurred and emended it to 'leman', meaning 'sweetheart'.

KEY FACTS

MAJOR PARTS: (*with percentages of lines/number of speeches/scenes on stage*) Sir Toby Belch (13%/152/10), Viola (13%/121/8), Olivia (12%/118/6), Feste (12%/104/7), Malvolio (11%/87/7), Orsino (9%/59/4), Sir Andrew (6%/88/8), Maria (6%/59/6), Sebastian (5%/31/5), Fabian (4%/51/4), Antonio (4%/26/4).

LINGUISTIC MEDIUM: 40% verse, 60% prose.

DATE: 1601: Performed at Middle Temple February 1602; not mentioned by Meres 1598; alludes to Anthony Sherley's visit to the Persian Sophy (1598–1601) and to a map first published in 1599; parodies the motif of self-love, double title, and use of word 'element' in Ben Jonson's *The Fountain of Self-Love, or Cynthia's Revels* (late 1600/early 1601), while a character in Jonson's *Poetaster* (performed later in 1601) seems to say that he has been to a performance of *Twelfth Night*.

SOURCES: Main plot adapted from the story of 'Apolonius and Silla' in Barnaby Riche's *Riche his Farewell to Military Profession* (1581), though the motif of the cross-dressed disguised 'page' wooing a lady on behalf of a master whom she loves herself is derived from a series of Italian comedies going back to *Gl'Ingannati* ('The Deceived'), an extremely bawdy play performed by 'The Academy of the Thunderstruck' in Siena (1537). The mistaking of twins is bred from Plautus' *Menaechmi* by way of Shakespeare's own *Comedy of Errors*. There is no clear source for the Sir Toby/Malvolio plot.

TEXT: First Folio of 1623 is only early printed text. Probably set from scribal copy, it is exceptionally free from errors and textual problems.

TWELFTH NIGHT, OR WHAT YOU WILL

ORSINO, Duke of Illyria

CURIO ⎫ courtiers attending
VALENTINE ⎭ upon Orsino

VIOLA, later disguised as Cesario

A Sea-CAPTAIN

SEBASTIAN, Viola's twin brother

ANTONIO, another sea-captain

OLIVIA, a Countess in Illyria

MARIA, her waiting-woman

SIR TOBY Belch, Olivia's kinsman

SIR ANDREW Aguecheek, companion
of Sir Toby

MALVOLIO, Olivia's steward

FABIAN, a member of Olivia's
household

FESTE the clown, Olivia's jester

Musicians, Sailors, Lords, Officers,
Servants, Attendants and a Priest

Act 1 Scene 1   *running scene 1*

Enter Orsino Duke of Illyria, Curio and other Lords   **Music plays**

ORSINO If music be the food of love, play on,
    Give me excess of it, that surfeiting,
    The appetite may sicken and so die.
    That strain again, it had a dying fall:
5   O, it came o'er my ear like the sweet sound
    That breathes upon a bank of violets,
    Stealing and giving odour. Enough, no more,
    'Tis not so sweet now as it was before.   **Music stops**
    O spirit of love, how quick and fresh art thou
10   That, notwithstanding thy capacity,
    Receiveth as the sea. Nought enters there,
    Of what validity and pitch soe'er,
    But falls into abatement and low price
    Even in a minute. So full of shapes is fancy
15   That it alone is high fantastical.
CURIO Will you go hunt, my lord?
ORSINO What, Curio?
CURIO The hart.
ORSINO Why so I do, the noblest that I have.
20   O, when mine eyes did see Olivia first,
    Methought she purged the air of pestilence.
    That instant was I turned into a hart,
    And my desires, like fell and cruel hounds,
    E'er since pursue me.
Enter Valentine
                 How now, what news from her?
25 **VALENTINE** So please my lord, I might not be admitted,
    But from her handmaid do return this answer:
    The element itself, till seven years' heat,

1.1 **Location:** *Illyria (country on the east of the Adriatic Sea; now Croatia). The entire action takes place here, moving between the households of Duke Orsino and Olivia, with occasional scenes in undetermined public places* **Orsino** Italian for 'bear-cub'; perhaps suggestive of immaturity **Curio** either 'curious' or 'courtly' (from the Italian for 'court'); may suggest fastidious affectation in dress and manners **2 surfeiting** overindulging (in food or sex) **3 appetite** hunger/sexual craving **4 dying fall** dropping cadence (plays on the sense of 'orgasm and detumescence') **5 sound** i.e. of a breeze **9 quick and fresh** sharp and eager, hungry **10 capacity** (small) size/ability to contain **11 as the sea** i.e. without limit **12 validity and pitch** worth and utmost elevation **13 abatement** diminution **14 shapes** imaginary forms **fancy** love/desire (plays on the sense of 'imagination') **15 alone...fantastical** is uniquely imaginative/delusory **18 hart** male deer (Orsino puns on 'heart') **21 pestilence** plague (often attributed to bad air) **23 fell** fierce **hounds...me** as in the classical myth of Actaeon, hunted down by his own hounds as punishment for gazing on the naked goddess Diana **Valentine** the name of the patron saint of lovers? **27 element** sky **years' heat** i.e. summers

Shall not behold her face at ample view,
But like a cloistress she will veilèd walk,
30 And water once a day her chamber round
With eye-offending brine — all this to season
A brother's dead love, which she would keep fresh
And lasting in her sad remembrance.
ORSINO O, she that hath a heart of that fine frame
35 To pay this debt of love but to a brother,
How will she love when the rich golden shaft
Hath killed the flock of all affections else
That live in her — when liver, brain and heart,
These sovereign thrones, are all supplied, and filled
40 Her sweet perfections with one self king!
Away before me, to sweet beds of flowers.
Love thoughts lie rich when canopied with bowers.

Exeunt

Act 1 Scene 2
running scene 2

Enter Viola, a Captain and Sailors

VIOLA What country, friends, is this?
CAPTAIN This is Illyria, lady.
VIOLA And what should I do in Illyria?
My brother he is in Elysium.
5 Perchance he is not drowned: what think you, sailors?
CAPTAIN It is perchance that you yourself were saved.
VIOLA O, my poor brother! And so perchance may he be.
CAPTAIN True, madam, and to comfort you with chance,
Assure yourself, after our ship did split,
10 When you and those poor number saved with you
Hung on our driving boat, I saw your brother,
Most provident in peril, bind himself —
Courage and hope both teaching him the practice —
To a strong mast that lived upon the sea,
15 Where, like Arion on the dolphin's back,

28 **ample** full, i.e. unveiled   29 **cloistress** nun   31 **eye-offending brine** stinging, salty tears   **season** preserve (with salt)   36 **golden shaft** i.e. arrow of Cupid (god of love)   37 **affections else** other feelings   38 **liver…heart** seats (**thrones**) of sexual passion, intellect and emotion   39 **supplied** filled/ satisfied   **filled…perfections** her perfect qualities are filled   40 **one self** one and the same   1.2 *Viola* Italian for 'violet', a flower that symbolized faithfulness and was thought to purge melancholy; also suggestive of musical instrument   4 **Elysium** the heaven of classical mythology   5 **Perchance** perhaps (the Captain shifts the sense to 'by chance')   8 **chance** the possibility of good fortune   11 **driving** storm-driven   12 **provident** foresighted/resourceful/fortunate   13 **practice** method   14 **lived** floated   15 **Arion** Greek musician who jumped overboard to escape being murdered and was carried to safety by a dolphin charmed by his music

I saw him hold acquaintance with the waves
So long as I could see.

VIOLA For saying so, there's gold.   *Gives money*
Mine own escape unfoldeth to my hope,
20   Whereto thy speech serves for authority,
The like of him. Know'st thou this country?

CAPTAIN Ay, madam, well, for I was bred and born
Not three hours' travel from this very place.

VIOLA Who governs here?

25 **CAPTAIN** A noble duke, in nature as in name.

VIOLA What is his name?

CAPTAIN Orsino.

VIOLA Orsino. I have heard my father name him.
He was a bachelor then.

30 **CAPTAIN** And so is now, or was so very late,
For but a month ago I went from hence,
And then 'twas fresh in murmur — as you know,
What great ones do, the less will prattle of —
That he did seek the love of fair Olivia.

35 **VIOLA** What's she?

CAPTAIN A virtuous maid, the daughter of a count
That died some twelvemonth since, then leaving her
In the protection of his son, her brother,
Who shortly also died, for whose dear love,
40   They say, she hath abjured the sight
And company of men.

VIOLA O that I served that lady,
And might not be delivered to the world
Till I had made mine own occasion mellow,
45   What my estate is.

CAPTAIN That were hard to compass,
Because she will admit no kind of suit,
No, not the duke's.

VIOLA There is a fair behaviour in thee, captain,
50   And though that nature with a beauteous wall
Doth oft close in pollution, yet of thee
I will believe thou hast a mind that suits
With this thy fair and outward character.

---

16 hold acquaintance with remain afloat upon   **19 unfoldeth . . . hope** encourages me to hope   **21 like of him** i.e. that he has also survived   **30 late** recently   **32 murmur** rumour   **33 What . . . of** whatever the aristocracy do, the lower classes gossip about it   **43 be . . . is** have my identity/rank revealed until I decide the time is ripe   **46 compass** bring about   **47 suit** petition/courtship   **48 not** not even   **49 fair behaviour** good conduct/promising appearance   **50 though that** though   **51 close in** enclose   **52 suits With** matches   **53 character** appearance

I prithee — and I'll pay thee bounteously —
55   Conceal me what I am, and be my aid
For such disguise as haply shall become
The form of my intent. I'll serve this duke.
Thou shalt present me as an eunuch to him.
It may be worth thy pains, for I can sing
60   And speak to him in many sorts of music
That will allow me very worth his service.
What else may hap, to time I will commit,
Only shape thou thy silence to my wit.

CAPTAIN   Be you his eunuch, and your mute I'll be:
65   When my tongue blabs, then let mine eyes not see.
VIOLA   I thank thee. Lead me on.   *Exeunt*

Act 1 Scene 3   *running scene 3*

Enter Sir Toby [Belch] and Maria

SIR TOBY   What a plague means my niece to take the
death of her brother thus? I am sure care's an enemy
to life.

MARIA   By my troth, Sir Toby, you must come in earlier
5   a-nights: your cousin, my lady, takes great
exceptions to your ill hours.

SIR TOBY   Why, let her except, before excepted.

MARIA   Ay, but you must confine yourself within the
modest limits of order.

10   SIR TOBY   Confine? I'll confine myself no finer than I am:
these clothes are good enough to drink in, and so be
these boots too. An they be not, let them hang
themselves in their own straps.

MARIA   That quaffing and drinking will undo you. I heard
15   my lady talk of it yesterday, and of a foolish knight
that you brought in one night here to be her wooer.

SIR TOBY   Who, Sir Andrew Aguecheek?

MARIA   Ay, he.

---

56 **haply...intent** may suit the shape of the purpose   58 **eunuch** male castrated to maintain a high
singing voice   61 **allow** prove   **worth** worthy of   62 **hap** happen, chance to occur   63 **wit** cunning
plan   1.3   1 **What a plague** an oath, like 'what the hell'   **niece** Toby may be Olivia's uncle, but 'niece'
could be used more generally for any female relative   2 **care** worry/grief   4 **troth** faith   5 **a-nights** at
night   **cousin** relative   6 **ill** antisocial   7 **except, before excepted** plays on the legal phrase *exceptis
excipiendis* ('with the aforementioned exceptions'); essentially Sir Toby says he does not care, Olivia may
object all she likes   9 **modest** moderate   10 **confine...finer** I won't restrain myself further/I won't dress
more finely   12 **An** if   14 **quaffing** copious drinking   17 **Aguecheek** suggesting thin face of one suffering
from a fever (ague)

SIR TOBY He's as tall a man as any's in Illyria.

20 MARIA What's that to th'purpose?

SIR TOBY Why, he has three thousand ducats a year.

MARIA Ay, but he'll have but a year in all these ducats: he's a very fool and a prodigal.

SIR TOBY Fie, that you'll say so! He plays o'th'viol-de-
25 gamboys, and speaks three or four languages word for word without book, and hath all the good gifts of nature.

MARIA He hath indeed, almost natural, for, besides that he's a fool, he's a great quarreller: and but that he
30 hath the gift of a coward to allay the gust he hath in quarrelling, 'tis thought among the prudent he would quickly have the gift of a grave.

SIR TOBY By this hand, they are scoundrels and subtractors that say so of him. Who are they?

35 MARIA They that add, moreover, he's drunk nightly in your company.

SIR TOBY With drinking healths to my niece. I'll drink to her as long as there is a passage in my throat and drink in Illyria. He's a coward and a coystrill that will
40 not drink to my niece till his brains turn o'th'toe like a parish top. What, wench? *Castiliano vulgo!* For here comes Sir Andrew Agueface.

Enter Sir Andrew [Aguecheek]

SIR ANDREW Sir Toby Belch. How now, Sir Toby Belch?

SIR TOBY Sweet Sir Andrew.

45 SIR ANDREW Bless you, fair shrew.   *To Maria*

MARIA And you too, sir.

SIR TOBY Accost, Sir Andrew, accost.

SIR ANDREW What's that?

SIR TOBY My niece's chambermaid.

50 SIR ANDREW Good Mistress Accost, I desire better acquaintance.

MARIA My name is Mary, sir.

---

19 tall brave/noble/of great height (Maria understands the latter meaning)   **any's** any (man) is
21 ducats gold coins (**three thousand** was a considerable annual income)   **22 he'll**…**ducats** he'll have
spent all his money in a year   **23 very** complete/veritable   **prodigal** excessively extravagant person
24 o'th'viol-de-gamboys the viol da gamba, a bass viol played held between the legs (often has sexual
connotations)   **26 without book** i.e. spontaneously, from memory   **28 natural** like an idiot   **30 allay**…
in reduce his taste for   **34 subtractors** detractors, slanderers   **39 coystrill** knave   **40 o'th'toe** head-over-
heels   **41 parish top** large spinning-top (kept rotating by being whipped), provided for parishioners'
entertainment   *Castiliano vulgo!* unclear Latin-Italian phrase; possibly 'Speak of the devil!'
42 Agueface playful variation of **Aguecheek**   **45 shrew** small mouse/troublesome one   **47 Accost**
approach/woo/grapple with   **49 chambermaid** female attendant

SIR ANDREW Good Mistress Mary Accost—

SIR TOBY You mistake, knight. 'Accost' is front her,
55 board her, woo her, assail her.

SIR ANDREW By my troth, I would not undertake her in
this company. Is that the meaning of 'accost'?

MARIA Fare you well, gentlemen.   *Starts to leave*

SIR TOBY An thou let part so, Sir Andrew, would thou
60 mightst never draw sword again.

SIR ANDREW An you part so, mistress, I would I might
never draw sword again. Fair lady, do you think you
have fools in hand?

MARIA Sir, I have not you by th'hand.

65 SIR ANDREW Marry, but you shall have, and here's my   *Gives her his*
hand.   *hand*

MARIA Now, sir, thought is free. I pray you bring your
hand to th'buttery-bar and let it drink.

SIR ANDREW Wherefore, sweetheart? What's your
70 metaphor?

MARIA It's dry, sir.

SIR ANDREW Why, I think so: I am not such an ass but I
can keep my hand dry. But what's your jest?

MARIA A dry jest, sir.

75 SIR ANDREW Are you full of them?

MARIA Ay, sir, I have them at my fingers' ends.   *Lets go of his hand*
Marry, now I let go your hand, I am barren.

Exit Maria

SIR TOBY O knight, thou lack'st a cup of canary. When
did I see thee so put down?

80 SIR ANDREW Never in your life, I think, unless you see
canary put me down. Methinks sometimes I have no
more wit than a Christian or an ordinary man has.
But I am a great eater of beef and I believe that does
harm to my wit.

---

54 front confront   **55 board** accost (sexual-naval metaphor referring to sex as attacking a ship)   **assail** attack, seduce   **56 undertake** approach/have sex with (literally, 'have her underneath me')   **in this company** in front of spectators   **59 An...so** if you let her leave in this way   **60 sword** symbol of gentlemanly status (with phallic connotations)   **63 in hand** to deal with (Maria takes the phrase literally; also plays on the idea of masturbation)   **65 Marry** by the virgin Mary   **67 thought is free** think what you like (proverbial)   **68 th'buttery-bar** the ledge created by opening the half-door of the buttery, with play on genitals   **69 Wherefore** why   **71 dry** thirsty/shrivelled/impotent (supposedly signified by a dry palm)   **72 I...dry** alludes to the proverb 'fools have wit enough to come in out of the rain'   **74 dry jest** stupid/ironic   **76 at...ends** always ready/literally by the hand   **77 barren** empty of jests and of Sir Andrew's hand   **78 canary** sweet wine from the Canary Islands; also continues play on impotence   **79 put down** snubbed (Sir Andrew plays on the senses of 'drunk/impotent')   **82 Christian** i.e. average man   **83 eater...wit** beef was thought to dull the intellect; wit may also signify 'penis' and beef 'whore', implying impotence as a result of veneral disease

85   SIR TOBY No question.
        SIR ANDREW An I thought that, I'd forswear it. I'll ride
            home tomorrow, Sir Toby.
        SIR TOBY *Pourquoi*, my dear knight?
        SIR ANDREW What is '*Pourquoi*'? Do or not do? I would I
90   had bestowed that time in the tongues that I have in
            fencing, dancing and bear-baiting. O, had I but
            followed the arts!
        SIR TOBY Then hadst thou had an excellent head of hair.
        SIR ANDREW Why, would that have mended my hair?
95   SIR TOBY Past question, for thou see'st it will not curl by
            nature.
        SIR ANDREW But it becomes me well enough, does't not?
        SIR TOBY Excellent. It hangs like flax on a distaff, and I
            hope to see a housewife take thee between her legs
100   and spin it off.
        SIR ANDREW Faith, I'll home tomorrow, Sir Toby. Your
            niece will not be seen, or if she be, it's four to one
            she'll none of me. The count himself here hard by
            woos her.
105   SIR TOBY She'll none o'th'count. She'll not match above
            her degree, neither in estate, years, nor wit; I have
            heard her swear't. Tut, there's life in't, man.
        SIR ANDREW I'll stay a month longer. I am a fellow
            o'th'strangest mind i'th'world: I delight in masques
110   and revels sometimes altogether.
        SIR TOBY Art thou good at these kickshawses, knight?
        SIR ANDREW As any man in Illyria, whatsoever he be,
            under the degree of my betters, and yet I will not
            compare with an old man.
115   SIR TOBY What is thy excellence in a galliard, knight?
        SIR ANDREW Faith, I can cut a caper.
        SIR TOBY And I can cut the mutton to't.

---

86 forswear it give it up   **88 *Pourquoi*** 'why' (French)   **90 tongues** foreign languages   **91 bear-baiting**
spectator sport in which a bear chained to a stake was attacked by dogs   **92 the arts** liberal arts/academic
learning   **93 head of hair** puns on **tongues** pronounced 'tongs', thus suggesting a barber's curling tongs
94 mended improved   **97 becomes** suits   **98 flax** yellow fibre   **distaff** staff used to spin flax
99 housewife woman who keeps house/prostitute   **take . . . off** treat Sir Andrew as a distaff and his hair as
flax to be spun/have sex with Sir Andrew, resulting in syphilitic hair loss   **103 none of me** have nothing to
do with me   **count** i.e. Duke Orsino   **hard** near   **106 degree** (social) position   **estate** status/fortune
wit intelligence   **107 life in't** still hope (proverbial)   **109 strangest** oddest/most extraordinary   **masques
and revels** courtly entertainments involving dancing   **111 kickshawses** trivial distractions/sexual
sweetmeats   **113 under . . . betters** except for my social superiors   **114 old man** expert   **115 galliard**
lively dance   **116 cut a caper** perform a leap/have sex   **117 cut . . . to't** plays on the sense of **caper** as a
berry used in sauce for **mutton**; also a prostitute

SIR ANDREW And I think I have the back-trick simply as
strong as any man in Illyria.

120 SIR TOBY Wherefore are these things hid? Wherefore
have these gifts a curtain before 'em? Are they like to
take dust, like Mistress Mall's picture? Why dost thou
not go to church in a galliard and come home in a
coranto? My very walk should be a jig, I would not so

125 much as make water but in a sink-a-pace. What dost
thou mean? Is it a world to hide virtues in? I did
think, by the excellent constitution of thy leg, it was
formed under the star of a galliard.

SIR ANDREW Ay, 'tis strong, and it does indifferent well

130 in a damned coloured stock. Shall we set about some
revels?

SIR TOBY What shall we do else? Were we not born
under Taurus?

SIR ANDREW Taurus? That's sides and heart.

135 SIR TOBY No, sir, it is legs and thighs. Let me see thee   *Sir Andrew*
caper. Ha? Higher, ha, ha! Excellent!   *Exeunt*   *dances*

Act 1 Scene 4   *running scene 4*

Enter Valentine and Viola [as Cesario] in man's attire

VALENTINE If the duke continue these favours towards
you, Cesario, you are like to be much advanced. He
hath known you but three days, and already you are
no stranger.

5 VIOLA You either fear his humour or my negligence, that
you call in question the continuance of his love. Is he
inconstant, sir, in his favours?

VALENTINE No, believe me.

Enter Duke [Orsino], Curio and Attendants

VIOLA I thank you. Here comes the count.

10 ORSINO Who saw Cesario, ho?

118 **back-trick** backward dance step/sex   121 **like to take** likely to gather   122 **Mistress Mall's picture**
i.e. a portrait protected from dust and light by a **curtain** (**Mall** is a diminutive of 'Mary')   123 **in** doing
124 **coranto** running dance   **jig** rapid, springing dance   125 **make water** urinate   **sink-a-pace**
cinquepace, a lively dance with five steps; may play on the sense of **sink** as 'sewer'   126 **virtues** talents
128 **star ... galliard** astrological influence favourable to dancing   129 **indifferent** moderately
130 **damned** damnably (the Folio reading 'dam'd' is defensible as an intensifier, but it could be emended to,
e.g., 'damson-coloured' or 'flame-coloured')   **stock** stocking   134 **Taurus ... heart** zodiacal signs were
thought to govern parts of the body   135 **legs and thighs** more usually Taurus was said to govern the neck
and throat   **1.4   2 Cesario** suggests 'little Caesar' and perhaps the idea of splitting/separating (as in
'Caesarean' and 'caesura')   **advanced** promoted   5 **humour** disposition/capriciousness

VIOLA On your attendance, my lord, here.

ORSINO Stand you awhile aloof.— Cesario,   *To Attendants, who*
    Thou know'st no less but all. I have unclasped   *stand aside*
    To thee the book even of my secret soul:
15   Therefore, good youth, address thy gait unto her,
    Be not denied access, stand at her doors,
    And tell them there thy fixèd foot shall grow
    Till thou have audience.

VIOLA Sure, my noble lord,
20   If she be so abandoned to her sorrow
    As it is spoke, she never will admit me.

ORSINO Be clamorous and leap all civil bounds
    Rather than make unprofited return.

VIOLA Say I do speak with her, my lord, what then?

25 **ORSINO** O, then unfold the passion of my love,
    Surprise her with discourse of my dear faith;
    It shall become thee well to act my woes.
    She will attend it better in thy youth
    Than in a nuncio's of more grave aspect.

30 **VIOLA** I think not so, my lord.

ORSINO Dear lad, believe it;
    For they shall yet belie thy happy years,
    That say thou art a man: Diana's lip
    Is not more smooth and rubious, thy small pipe
35   Is as the maiden's organ, shrill and sound,
    And all is semblative a woman's part.
    I know thy constellation is right apt
    For this affair.— Some four or five attend him.   *To Attendants*
    All, if you will, for I myself am best
40   When least in company. Prosper well in this,
    And thou shalt live as freely as thy lord,
    To call his fortunes thine.

VIOLA I'll do my best
    To woo your lady.— Yet, a barful strife!   *Aside*
45   Whoe'er I woo, myself would be his wife.   *Exeunt*

---

11 On your attendance ready to serve you   **12 aloof** to one side   **13 no ... all** i.e. everything
15 address thy gait direct your steps   **17 them** i.e. Olivia's servants   **grow** i.e. take root   **18 audience**
reception by Olivia   **21 spoke** said, rumoured   **22 civil bounds** bounds of civilized behaviour
26 Surprise ambush, take unawares   **faith** faithful love   **27 become** suit   **28 attend** listen, pay attention
to   **29 nuncio's** messenger's   **aspect** appearance   **31 lad** servant/young man   **32 belie** deceive
33 Diana's lip Diana was the Roman goddess of the moon, hunting and chastity; in view of 'pipe' and
'organ', lip may play on 'nether lip' (labia)   **34 rubious** ruby-red   **pipe** voice/penis   **35 shrill and sound**
high-pitched and unbroken   **36 is semblative** resembles   **part** attributes/role/sexual **organ**
37 constellation disposition determined by the stars   **41 freely** independently   **44 barful strife** effort full
of hindrances

Act 1 Scene 5   *running scene 5*

Enter Maria and Clown [Feste]

MARIA Nay, either tell me where thou hast been, or I will
      not open my lips so wide as a bristle may enter in
      way of thy excuse. My lady will hang thee for thy
      absence.

5   FESTE Let her hang me: he that is well hanged in this
      world needs to fear no colours.

MARIA Make that good.

FESTE He shall see none to fear.

MARIA A good lenten answer. I can tell thee where that
10   saying was born, of 'I fear no colours.'

FESTE Where, good Mistress Mary?

MARIA In the wars, and that may you be bold to say in
      your foolery.

FESTE Well, God give them wisdom that have it, and
15   those that are fools, let them use their talents.

MARIA Yet you will be hanged for being so long absent,
      or, to be turned away, is not that as good as a
      hanging to you?

FESTE Many a good hanging prevents a bad marriage,
20   and, for turning away, let summer bear it out.

MARIA You are resolute, then?

FESTE Not so, neither. But I am resolved on two points.

MARIA That if one break, the other will hold, or if both
      break, your gaskins fall.

25   FESTE Apt, in good faith, very apt. Well, go thy way. If
      Sir Toby would leave drinking, thou wert as witty a
      piece of Eve's flesh as any in Illyria.

MARIA Peace, you rogue, no more o'that. Here comes my
      lady: make your excuse wisely, you were best. *[Exit]*
      Enter Lady Olivia with Malvolio [and Attendants]

30   FESTE Wit, an't be thy will, put me into good fooling!   *Aside*
      Those wits, that think they have thee, do very oft

1.5 *Feste* From Latin or Italian, *festa* ('feast' or 'festival'), an appropriate name for a fool/clown   **2 in** by   **5 well
hanged** plays on the sense of 'with a large penis'   **6 no colours** i.e. nothing (literally, military flags); puns
on 'collars' (nooses)   **7 Make that good** justify yourself   **8 He . . . fear** i.e. a dead man cannot see (enemy
colours)   **9 lenten** meagre (Lent, the time of fasting, was especially associated with puritanism)   **12 bold**
confident/certain   **17 turned away** dismissed from service   **19 Many . . . marriage** proverbial; **good
hanging** may continue play on the sense of 'large penis'   **20 for** as for   **let . . . out** i.e. good weather will
make dismissal more bearable   **22 points** matters (Maria plays on the sense of 'laces used to hold up
breeches')   **24 gaskins** breeches   **25 Apt** quick, witty   **If . . . drinking** either never, or suggesting that
Maria and Sir Toby would be a good match   **27 Eve's flesh** woman   **29 were best** are best advised
Malvolio 'ill-will' (Latin)   **30 an't** if it

prove fools, and I that am sure I lack thee, may pass
for a wise man. For what says Quinapalus? 'Better a
witty fool than a foolish wit.'— God bless thee, lady.   *To Olivia*

35 OLIVIA Take the fool away.   *To Attendants*

FESTE Do you not hear, fellows? Take away the lady.

OLIVIA Go to, you're a dry fool. I'll no more of you.
Besides, you grow dishonest.

FESTE Two faults, Madonna, that drink and good
40   counsel will amend. For give the dry fool drink,
then is the fool not dry: bid the dishonest man mend
himself. If he mend, he is no longer dishonest; if he
cannot, let the botcher mend him. Anything that's
mended is but patched: virtue that transgresses is but
45   patched with sin, and sin that amends is but patched
with virtue. If that this simple syllogism will serve, so.
If it will not, what remedy? As there is no true
cuckold but calamity, so beauty's a flower. The lady
bade take away the fool: therefore, I say again, take
50   her away.

OLIVIA Sir, I bade them take away you.

FESTE Misprision in the highest degree! Lady, *cucullus
non facit monachum*: that's as much to say as I wear
not motley in my brain. Good madonna, give me
55   leave to prove you a fool.

OLIVIA Can you do it?

FESTE Dexteriously, good madonna.

OLIVIA Make your proof.

FESTE I must catechize you for it, madonna. Good my
60   mouse of virtue, answer me.

OLIVIA Well, sir, for want of other idleness, I'll bide your
proof.

FESTE Good madonna, why mourn'st thou?

OLIVIA Good fool, for my brother's death.

---

33 Quinapalus an invented authority, perhaps playing on French *qui n'a pas lu* ('unread') or mock Italian 'him on the stick' (the face on the fool's bauble)   **37 Go to** expression of impatient dismissal   **dry** dull   **38 dishonest** undutiful   **39 Madonna** 'my lady' (Italian)   **41 dry** dull/thirsty   **mend** improve; later plays on the sense of 'repair'   **43 botcher** mender of clothes and shoes   **44 patched** simply mended, covered up; also alludes to the fool's multicoloured costume   **46 simple** uncomplicated/foolish   **syllogism** reasoning based on two premises (here those concerning virtue and sin)   **so** well and good   **47 no . . . calamity** i.e. one married to calamity will always be faithless   **48 cuckold** man with an unfaithful wife   **beauty's a flower** i.e. it will fade; Feste advises Olivia to make the most of her youth and beauty, rather than shutting herself away and refusing to marry   **52 Misprision** error/wrongful arrest   *cucullus . . . monachum* 'a hood does not make a monk' (Latin)   **54 motley** multicoloured clothing worn by professional fools   **55 leave** permission   **57 Dexteriously** skilfully   **59 catechize** cross-examine (literally, form of Church instruction in which a person answers a set of questions about the Christian faith)   **Good . . . virtue** my good virtuous mouse; playful term of endearment   **61 idleness** pastime   **bide** await/endure

65 FESTE I think his soul is in hell, madonna.

OLIVIA I know his soul is in heaven, fool.

FESTE The more fool, madonna, to mourn for your brother's soul being in heaven. Take away the fool, gentlemen.

70 OLIVIA What think you of this fool, Malvolio? Doth he not mend?

MALVOLIO Yes, and shall do till the pangs of death shake him. Infirmity, that decays the wise, doth ever make the better fool.

75 FESTE God send you, sir, a speedy infirmity, for the better increasing your folly! Sir Toby will be sworn that I am no fox, but he will not pass his word for twopence that you are no fool.

OLIVIA How say you to that, Malvolio?

80 MALVOLIO I marvel your ladyship takes delight in such a barren rascal. I saw him put down the other day with an ordinary fool that has no more brain than a stone. Look you now, he's out of his guard already. Unless you laugh and minister occasion to him, he is

85 gagged. I protest, I take these wise men, that crow so at these set kind of fools, no better than the fools' zanies.

OLIVIA O, you are sick of self-love, Malvolio, and taste with a distempered appetite. To be generous, guiltless

90 and of free disposition is to take those things for bird-bolts that you deem cannon-bullets. There is no slander in an allowed fool, though he do nothing but rail; nor no railing in a known discreet man, though he do nothing but reprove.

95 FESTE Now Mercury endue thee with leasing, for thou speak'st well of fools.

Enter Maria

MARIA Madam, there is at the gate a young gentleman much desires to speak with you.

OLIVIA From the Count Orsino, is it?

---

71 mend improve (Malvolio shifts the sense to 'grow (more foolish)'   **77 no fox** not cunning   **pass** give   **81 barren** dull-witted   **put down** defeated   **with** by   **82 ordinary fool** unexceptional fool/fool performing at an inn (**ordinary**)/natural idiot   **stone** may also refer to Stone, an Elizabethan tavern fool   **83 out...guard** defenceless (fencing term), i.e. lacking a witty reply   **84 minister occasion** provide opportunity (for fooling)   **85 protest** declare   **crow** laugh raucously   **86 set** unspontaneous   **87 zanies** assistants   **88 of** with   **89 distempered** unbalanced   **90 free** generous   **bird-bolts** blunt arrows for shooting birds   **92 allowed** licensed   **93 rail** rant   **discreet** prudent   **94 reprove** express disapproval   **95 Mercury...leasing** may **Mercury**, god of deception, make you good at lying

100 **MARIA** I know not, madam. 'Tis a fair young man, and
well attended.

OLIVIA Who of my people hold him in delay?

MARIA Sir Toby, madam, your kinsman.

OLIVIA Fetch him off, I pray you. He speaks nothing but
105 madman. Fie on him!— *[Exit Maria]*
Go you, Malvolio; if it be a suit from the count, I am
sick, or not at home. What you will, to dismiss it.—
Exit Malvolio
Now you see, sir, how your fooling grows old, and
people dislike it.

110 **FESTE** Thou hast spoke for us, madonna, as if thy eldest
son should be a fool, whose skull Jove cram with
brains, for — here he comes —
Enter Sir Toby
one of thy kin has a most weak pia mater.

OLIVIA By mine honour, half drunk.— What is he at the   *To Sir Toby*
115 gate, cousin?

SIR TOBY A gentleman.

OLIVIA A gentleman? What gentleman?

SIR TOBY 'Tis a gentleman here— a plague o'these *Belches/To Feste*
pickle herring!— How now, sot?

120 **FESTE** Good Sir Toby!

OLIVIA Cousin, cousin, how have you come so early by
this lethargy?

SIR TOBY Lechery? I defy lechery. There's one at the
gate.

125 **OLIVIA** Ay, marry, what is he?

SIR TOBY Let him be the devil, an he will, I care not. Give
me faith, say I. Well, it's all one.   *Exit*

OLIVIA What's a drunken man like, fool?

FESTE Like a drowned man, a fool and a madman: one
130 draught above heat makes him a fool, the second
mads him, and a third drowns him.

OLIVIA Go thou and seek the crowner, and let him sit
o'my coz, for he's in the third degree of drink: he's
drowned. Go look after him.

---

105 **madman** i.e. rubbish, gibberish   **Fie** expression of impatience or disgust   107 **What you will** whatever
you want to say   108 **old** stale   111 **should be** were   **Jove** Roman king of the gods   113 **pia mater**
brain (literally, soft membrane enclosing it)   119 **sot** fool/drunkard   122 **lethargy** (drunken) state
123 **one** someone   127 **faith** i.e. to defy the devil   **it's all one** it doesn't matter   129 **one...heat** one
drink beyond that which would warm him   131 **drowns** makes him excessively drunk/unintelligible/
unconscious   132 **crowner** coroner   **sit o'my coz** hold an inquest on my kinsman

135 **FESTE** He is but mad yet, madonna, and the fool shall
      look to the madman.   [*Exit*]
      Enter Malvolio
      MALVOLIO Madam, yond young fellow swears he will
      speak with you. I told him you were sick, he takes on
      him to understand so much, and therefore comes to
140   speak with you. I told him you were asleep — he
      seems to have a foreknowledge of that too — and
      therefore comes to speak with you. What is to be said
      to him, lady? He's fortified against any denial.
      OLIVIA Tell him he shall not speak with me.
145 **MALVOLIO** He's been told so, and he says he'll stand at
      your door like a sheriff's post, and be the supporter to
      a bench, but he'll speak with you.
      OLIVIA What kind o'man is he?
      MALVOLIO Why, of mankind.
150 **OLIVIA** What manner of man?
      MALVOLIO Of very ill manner. He'll speak with you, will
      you or no.
      OLIVIA Of what personage and years is he?
      MALVOLIO Not yet old enough for a man, nor young
155   enough for a boy. As a squash is before 'tis a peascod,
      or a codling when 'tis almost an apple: 'tis with him
      in standing water, between boy and man. He is very
      well-favoured and he speaks very shrewishly. One
      would think his mother's milk were scarce out of
160   him.
      OLIVIA Let him approach. Call in my gentlewoman.
      MALVOLIO Gentlewoman, my lady calls.   *Exit*
      Enter Maria
      OLIVIA Give me my veil. Come, throw it o'er my face.
      We'll once more hear Orsino's embassy.   *She is veiled*
      Enter Viola [and Attendants]
165 **VIOLA** The honourable lady of the house, which is she?
      OLIVIA Speak to me, I shall answer for her. Your will?
      VIOLA Most radiant, exquisite and unmatchable beauty
      — I pray you tell me if this be the lady of the house,

---

137 yond yonder, that   **138 takes . . . understand** understands   **146 sheriff's post** decorated post
denoting authority, fixed in front of the sheriff's door   **supporter . . . bench** furniture support (**bench** plays
on the sense of 'court of justice')   **149 of mankind** i.e. ordinary   **151 ill manner** i.e. impolite   **will . . . no**
whether you want to or not   **153 personage** appearance   **155 squash** unripe pea-pod (**peascod**, allusive
of genitals – a humorous reversal of 'codpiece', a bag worn over the opening at the front of a man's
breeches)   **156 codling** unripe apple, plays on 'cod' meaning 'scrotum'   **157 standing water** at the turn
of the tide   **158 well-favoured** good-looking   **shrewishly** sharply/shrilly   **164 embassy** message/
ambassador

for I never saw her. I would be loath to cast away my
170 speech, for besides that it is excellently well penned, I
have taken great pains to con it. Good beauties, let
me sustain no scorn; I am very comptible, even to the
least sinister usage.

OLIVIA Whence came you, sir?

175 **VIOLA** I can say little more than I have studied, and that
question's out of my part. Good gentle one, give me
modest assurance, if you be the lady of the house,
that I may proceed in my speech.

OLIVIA Are you a comedian?

180 **VIOLA** No, my profound heart. And yet, by the very fangs
of malice, I swear I am not that I play. Are you the
lady of the house?

OLIVIA If I do not usurp myself, I am.

VIOLA Most certain, if you are she, you do usurp yourself,
185 for what is yours to bestow is not yours to reserve.
But this is from my commission. I will on with my
speech in your praise, and then show you the heart
of my message.

OLIVIA Come to what is important in't. I forgive you the
190 praise.

VIOLA Alas, I took great pains to study it, and 'tis
poetical.

OLIVIA It is the more like to be feigned. I pray you keep it
in. I heard you were saucy at my gates, and allowed
195 your approach rather to wonder at you than to hear
you. If you be not mad, be gone. If you have reason,
be brief. 'Tis not that time of moon with me to make
one in so skipping a dialogue.

MARIA Will you hoist sail, sir? Here lies your way.

200 **VIOLA** No, good swabber, I am to hull here a little longer.
Some mollification for your giant, sweet lady; tell me
your mind, I am a messenger.

169 cast away waste   **170 penned** written   **171 con** learn by heart   **172 sustain** endure   **comptible** sensitive   **173 sinister** impolite   **175 studied** learned, memorized   **176 out . . . part** not within my brief   **177 modest** reasonable   **179 comedian** actor   **180 my profound heart** upon my soul/(to Olivia) my wise lady   **181 that I play** the character I perform   **183 usurp** counterfeit (Viola shifts the sense to 'assume unjust authority over')   **185 what . . . reserve** i.e. Olivia should not withhold herself from love and marriage   **186 from** outside, not part of   **on** go on   **189 forgive** excuse from repeating   **193 feigned** fictional/insincere   **it in** it to yourself   **194 saucy** impudent   **195 wonder** marvel   **196 If . . . brief** i.e. if Viola has any sense at all she should go; any sensible message must be conveyed quickly   **197 'Tis . . . me** I am not a lunatic, i.e. not affected by the moon's changes   **make one** take part   **198 skipping** frivolous, mad   **199 hoist sail** i.e. prepare to leave   **200 swabber** sailor who washes the deck   **hull** float, with sails furled   **201 Some mollification** please pacify/I have pacified   **giant** i.e. Maria; a joke about Maria's small size and/or Maria resembles a giant in a romance tale who guarded a lady

OLIVIA Sure, you have some hideous matter to deliver,
when the courtesy of it is so fearful. Speak your office.
205 VIOLA It alone concerns your ear. I bring no overture of
war, no taxation of homage; I hold the olive in my
hand. My words are as full of peace as matter.
OLIVIA Yet you began rudely. What are you? What
would you?
210 VIOLA The rudeness that hath appeared in me have I
learned from my entertainment. What I am, and
what I would, are as secret as maidenhead: to your
ears, divinity: to any other's, profanation.
OLIVIA Give us the place alone. We will hear this divinity.
[*Exeunt Maria and Attendants*]
215   Now, sir, what is your text?
VIOLA Most sweet lady—
OLIVIA A comfortable doctrine, and much may be said of
it. Where lies your text?
VIOLA In Orsino's bosom.
220 OLIVIA In his bosom? In what chapter of his bosom?
VIOLA To answer by the method, in the first of his heart.
OLIVIA O, I have read it: it is heresy. Have you no more to
say?
VIOLA Good madam, let me see your face.
225 OLIVIA Have you any commission from your lord to
negotiate with my face? You are now out of your
text. But we will draw the curtain and show you the
picture. Look you, sir, such a one I was this present.   *Unveils*
Is't not well done?
230 VIOLA Excellently done, if God did all.
OLIVIA 'Tis in grain, sir, 'twill endure wind and weather.
VIOLA 'Tis beauty truly blent, whose red and white
Nature's own sweet and cunning hand laid on.
Lady, you are the cruell'st she alive,

204 **courtesy** introduction, preamble/etiquette   **fearful** frightening, alarming   **Speak your office** perform
your task, deliver your speech   205 **overture** disclosure   206 **taxation of homage** demand for money
on behalf of a superior lord   **olive** olive branch, symbol of peace   207 **matter** real substance   208 **rudely**
i.e. by being saucy at the gates   211 **entertainment** reception   212 **maidenhead** virginity   213 **divinity**
sacred   **profanation** blasphemy   215 **text** theme/topic drawn from the Bible for discussion in a
sermon   217 **comfortable** comforting   219 **bosom** heart   220 **chapter** as of the Bible   221 **answer**...
method continue the metaphor   226 **out of** straying from   227 **curtain** i.e. veil covering Olivia's face
(**picture**)   228 **such**...**present** i.e. here I am (Olivia speaks of her face as if it was a recent portrait)
230 **if**...**all** i.e. if all Olivia's beauty is natural, rather than cosmetic or touched up by the metaphorical
painter   231 **in grain** indelible, i.e. all natural   232 **truly blent** genuinely blended/realistically painted
red and white i.e. lips (or rosy cheeks) and skin   233 **cunning** skilful   234 **she** lady

235 If you will lead these graces to the grave
    And leave the world no copy.
  OLIVIA O, sir, I will not be so hard-hearted. I will give out
    divers schedules of my beauty. It shall be inventoried,
    and every particle and utensil labelled to my will: as,
240 *item*, two lips, indifferent red: *item*, two grey eyes,
    with lids to them: *item*, one neck, one chin and so
    forth. Were you sent hither to praise me?
  VIOLA I see you what you are, you are too proud.
    But if you were the devil, you are fair.
245 My lord and master loves you. O, such love
    Could be but recompensed, though you were crowned
    The nonpareil of beauty!
  OLIVIA How does he love me?
  VIOLA With adorations, fertile tears,
250 With groans that thunder love, with sighs of fire.
  OLIVIA Your lord does know my mind: I cannot love him.
    Yet I suppose him virtuous, know him noble,
    Of great estate, of fresh and stainless youth;
    In voices well divulged, free, learned and valiant,
255 And in dimension and the shape of nature
    A gracious person; but yet I cannot love him.
    He might have took his answer long ago.
  VIOLA If I did love you in my master's flame,
    With such a suff'ring, such a deadly life,
260 In your denial I would find no sense,
    I would not understand it.
  OLIVIA Why, what would you?
  VIOLA Make me a willow cabin at your gate,
    And call upon my soul within the house,
265 Write loyal cantons of contemnèd love
    And sing them loud even in the dead of night,
    Hallow your name to the reverberate hills
    And make the babbling gossip of the air
    Cry out 'Olivia!' O, you should not rest

235 graces beauties   **236 copy** replica in the form of a child (Olivia plays on the sense of 'list') **238 divers schedules** several inventories   **inventoried** itemized   **239 utensil** article, feature **240 indifferent** adequately   **242 praise** puns on 'appraise', i.e. evaluate   **244 if** even if   **246 but recompensed, though** no more than repaid, even if   **247 nonpareil** paragon   **249 fertile** abundant **252 suppose** consider   **254 In ... divulged** well-regarded in popular opinion   **free** honourable/generous **255 dimension ... nature** physical form   **256 gracious** graceful, attractive   **258 flame** passion **259 deadly** death-like   **263 willow cabin** shelter made from willow branches, a symbol of unrequited love   **264 my soul** i.e. Olivia   **265 cantons** songs   **contemnèd** despised, rejected   **267 Hallow** shout/ bless   **reverberate** echoing   **268 babbling ... air** like that of Echo, whose unrequited love for Narcissus meant she wasted away to a mere voice   **gossip** chatter

270   Between the elements of air and earth,
    But you should pity me!
  OLIVIA You might do much. What is your parentage?
  VIOLA Above my fortunes, yet my state is well:
    I am a gentleman.
275 OLIVIA Get you to your lord.
    I cannot love him. Let him send no more,
    Unless, perchance, you come to me again,
    To tell me how he takes it. Fare you well:
    I thank you for your pains. Spend this for me.   *Offers a purse*
280 VIOLA I am no fee'd post, lady; keep your purse.
    My master, not myself, lacks recompense.
    Love make his heart of flint that you shall love,
    And let your fervour, like my master's, be
    Placed in contempt! Farewell, fair cruelty.   *Exit*
285 OLIVIA 'What is your parentage?'
    'Above my fortunes, yet my state is well;
    I am a gentleman.' I'll be sworn thou art.
    Thy tongue, thy face, thy limbs, actions and spirit,
    Do give thee five-fold blazon. Not too fast. Soft, soft!
290   Unless the master were the man. How now?
    Even so quickly may one catch the plague?
    Methinks I feel this youth's perfections
    With an invisible and subtle stealth
    To creep in at mine eyes. Well, let it be.
295   What ho, Malvolio!
  Enter Malvolio
  MALVOLIO Here, madam, at your service.
  OLIVIA Run after that same peevish messenger,
    The county's man. He left this ring behind him,   *Gives a ring*
    Would I or not. Tell him I'll none of it.
300   Desire him not to flatter with his lord,
    Nor hold him up with hopes. I am not for him.
    If that the youth will come this way tomorrow,
    I'll give him reasons for't. Hie thee, Malvolio.
  MALVOLIO Madam, I will.   *Exit*

---

273 fortunes position as a servant   **state** social status   **well** satisfactory   **280 fee'd post** hired messenger   **282 Love . . . love** may Love harden the heart of whomever you fall in love with   **289 blazon** heraldic coat of arms, which could only be displayed by a gentleman   **Soft** wait a moment   **290 the . . . man** i.e. Orsino and Cesario could change places   **man** servant   **291 catch the plague** i.e. fall in love   **297 peevish** headstrong   **298 county's** count's, i.e. Duke Orsino's   **299 Would I** whether I wanted it   **300 Desire** ask   **flatter with** i.e. encourage   **301 hold . . . hopes** sustain him with false expectations   **303 Hie** hasten

305 OLIVIA I do I know not what, and fear to find
       Mine eye too great a flatterer for my mind.
       Fate, show thy force. Ourselves we do not owe.
       What is decreed must be, and be this so.   [*Exit*]

Act 2 Scene 1   *running scene 6*

Enter Antonio and Sebastian

ANTONIO Will you stay no longer? Nor will you not that I
       go with you?
SEBASTIAN By your patience, no. My stars shine darkly
       over me; the malignancy of my fate might perhaps
5   distemper yours; therefore I shall crave of you your
       leave that I may bear my evils alone. It were a bad
       recompense for your love to lay any of them on you.
ANTONIO Let me yet know of you whither you are
       bound.
10   SEBASTIAN No, sooth, sir: my determinate voyage is
       mere extravagancy. But I perceive in you so excellent
       a touch of modesty that you will not extort from me
       what I am willing to keep in. Therefore it charges me
       in manners the rather to express myself. You must
15   know of me then, Antonio, my name is Sebastian,
       which I called Roderigo. My father was that
       Sebastian of Messaline whom I know you have
       heard of. He left behind him myself and a sister, both
       born in an hour. If the heavens had been pleased,
20   would we had so ended. But you, sir, altered that, for
       some hour before you took me from the breach of the
       sea was my sister drowned.
ANTONIO Alas the day!
SEBASTIAN A lady, sir, though it was said she much
25   resembled me, was yet of many accounted beautiful.
       But though I could not with such estimable wonder
       overfar believe that, yet thus far I will boldly publish
       her: she bore a mind that envy could not but call fair.

306 **Mine . . . mind** my eyes (through which love enters) may have betrayed my reason   307 **owe** own
2.1   1 **Nor . . . not** do you not wish   3 **patience** permission   **darkly** ominously   4 **malignancy** evil
influence   5 **distemper** spoil, unbalance   **crave** entreat   6 **leave** permission   **evils** misfortunes
10 **sooth** (in) truth   **determinate** intended   11 **extravagancy** wandering   12 **modesty** propriety
13 **am . . . in** wish to keep secret   **it . . . manners** politeness compels me   14 **express** reveal
16 **called** said was   17 **Messaline** unclear, possibly Marseilles or Messina, or invented by Shakespeare
19 **an hour** the same hour (they are twins)   21 **some** about an   **breach** breaking waves   26 **estimable**
wonder admiring judgement   27 **overfar** too greatly   **publish** speak openly of/celebrate   28 **envy** malice

She is drowned already, sir, with salt water, though I
30   seem to drown her remembrance again with more.
ANTONIO Pardon me, sir, your bad entertainment.
SEBASTIAN O, good Antonio, forgive me your trouble.
ANTONIO If you will not murder me for my love, let me be
your servant.
35   **SEBASTIAN** If you will not undo what you have done,
that is, kill him whom you have recovered, desire it
not. Fare ye well at once. My bosom is full of
kindness, and I am yet so near the manners of my
mother that upon the least occasion more mine eyes
40   will tell tales of me. I am bound to the Count Orsino's
court. Farewell.   *Exit*
ANTONIO The gentleness of all the gods go with thee!
I have many enemies in Orsino's court,
Else would I very shortly see thee there.
45   But come what may, I do adore thee so,
That danger shall seem sport, and I will go.   *Exit*

Act 2 Scene 2   *running scene 7*

Enter Viola and Malvolio at several doors

MALVOLIO Were not you ev'n now with the Countess
Olivia?
VIOLA Even now, sir, on a moderate pace I have since
arrived but hither.
5   **MALVOLIO** She returns this ring to you, sir. You might   *Shows a ring*
have saved me my pains, to have taken it away
yourself. She adds, moreover, that you should put
your lord into a desperate assurance she will none of
him. And one thing more, that you be never so hardy
10   to come again in his affairs, unless it be to report your
lord's taking of this. Receive it so.
VIOLA She took the ring of me. I'll none of it.
MALVOLIO Come, sir, you peevishly threw it to her, and
her will is, it should be so returned. If it be worth   *Throws it on*

30 **more** i.e. tears   31 **entertainment** reception (for one so worthy)   32 **your trouble** the trouble I put you
to   33 **murder…love** i.e. by making me leave you   36 **recovered** rescued, brought back to life
38 **kindness** tenderness/natural affection (for my sister)   **yet** still   **manners…mother** i.e. a womanish
inclination to weep   40 **tell…me** i.e. betray my feelings by crying   42 **gentleness** good favour
44 **Else** otherwise   46 **sport** recreation   2.2   1 **ev'n** just   3 **on** at   4 **but hither** only this far
8 **desperate assurance** hopeless certainty   9 **hardy** bold   10 **in his affairs** on his business   11 **taking of
this** understanding of this message/reception of the ring   **it** the ring   13 **peevishly** wilfully, foolishly
14 **so** in the same manner, i.e. thrown

15   stooping for, there it lies in your eye. If not, be it his
          that finds it.   *Exit*
      VIOLA I left no ring with her. What means this lady?
          Fortune forbid my outside have not charmed her!
          She made good view of me, indeed so much
20   That methought her eyes had lost her tongue,
          For she did speak in starts distractedly.
          She loves me, sure. The cunning of her passion
          Invites me in this churlish messenger.
          None of my lord's ring? Why, he sent her none;
25   I am the man. If it be so, as 'tis,
          Poor lady, she were better love a dream.
          Disguise, I see, thou art a wickedness,
          Wherein the pregnant enemy does much.
          How easy is it for the proper-false
30   In women's waxen hearts to set their forms!
          Alas, our frailty is the cause, not we,
          For such as we are made of, such we be.
          How will this fadge? My master loves her dearly,
          And I, poor monster, fond as much on him,
35   And she, mistaken, seems to dote on me.
          What will become of this? As I am man,
          My state is desperate for my master's love.
          As I am woman — now alas the day! —
          What thriftless sighs shall poor Olivia breathe?
40   O time, thou must untangle this, not I.
          It is too hard a knot for me t'untie.   [*Exit*]

Act 2 Scene 3   *running scene 8*

Enter Sir Toby and Sir Andrew

      SIR TOBY Approach, Sir Andrew. Not to be abed after
          midnight is to be up betimes, and *diluculo surgere*,
          thou know'st—
      SIR ANDREW Nay, by my troth I know not, but I know to
5   be up late is to be up late.

---

15 **eye** plain sight   18 **outside** appearance   19 **made ... of** had a good look at   20 **lost** made her lose
21 **starts** bursts   **distractedly** with agitation/madly   23 **in** by way of   **churlish** blunt, ungracious
26 **were better** would be better off   28 **pregnant** resourceful   **enemy** probably Satan   29 **proper-false**
attractive but deceitful (men)   30 **set their forms** make their impressions (like seals in wax)   31 **our ... be**
i.e. because women are made of frail material, we are weak   33 **fadge** turn out   34 **monster** unnatural
creature (being both man and woman)   **fond** dote   37 **state ... for** situation is hopeless with regard to
39 **thriftless** unprofitable   2.3   1 **Approach** come   2 **betimes** early   *diluculo surgere*
(... *saluberrimum est*) 'to get up early is most healthy' (Latin proverb)

SIR TOBY A false conclusion. I hate it as an unfilled can.
To be up after midnight and to go to bed then is early:
so that to go to bed after midnight is to go to bed
betimes. Does not our lives consist of the four
10 elements?

SIR ANDREW Faith, so they say, but I think it rather
consists of eating and drinking.

SIR TOBY Thou'rt a scholar; let us therefore eat and
drink. Marian, I say, a stoup of wine!

Enter Clown [Feste]

15 **SIR ANDREW** Here comes the fool, i'faith.

FESTE How now, my hearts! Did you never see the
picture of 'we three'?

SIR TOBY Welcome, ass. Now let's have a catch.

SIR ANDREW By my troth the fool has an excellent
20 breast. I had rather than forty shillings I had such a
leg, and so sweet a breath to sing, as the fool has. In
sooth thou wast in very gracious fooling last night,
when thou spokest of Pigrogromitus, of the Vapians
passing the equinoctial of Queubus. 'Twas very good,
25 i'faith. I sent thee sixpence for thy leman. Hadst it?

FESTE I did impeticos thy gratillity, for Malvolio's nose is
no whipstock. My lady has a white hand, and the
Myrmidons are no bottle-ale houses.

SIR ANDREW Excellent. Why, this is the best fooling,
30 when all is done. Now, a song.

SIR TOBY Come on, there is sixpence for you. Let's have   *Gives a coin*
a song.   *to Feste*

SIR ANDREW There's a testril of me too. If one knight   *Gives another*
give a—   *coin*

35 **FESTE** Would you have a love song, or a song of good
life?

SIR TOBY A love song, a love song.

---

6 can drinking vessel   **9 lives** i.e. living beings (Sir Andrew interprets as 'way of life')   **four elements**
earth, air, fire and water, from which everything was thought to be made   **14 Marian** variant of Mary/
Maria   **stoup** drinking vessel/measure of alcohol   **16 hearts** fine friends   **17 picture . . . three** captioned
picture showing two fools or asses, so that the spectator is the third   **18 catch** musical round   **20 breast**
set of lungs, singing voice   **21 leg** for dancing, or bowing before singing   **22 thou wast** you were
23 Pigrogromitus . . . Queubus words invented by Feste as examples of his feigned wisdom   **equinoctial**
equator   **25 leman** sweetheart   **Hadst it?** Did you receive it?   **26 impeticos** i.e. pocket up   **gratillity**
gratuity (another invented word)   **27 whipstock** whip-handle   **28 Myrmidons** Achilles' followers;
possible play on 'Mermaid Inn', a tavern in Shakespeare's London   **bottle-ale houses** low-class
taverns   **33 testril** sixpenny coin from   **35 song . . . life** drinking song (Sir Andrew interprets **good** as
'virtuous, moral')

SIR ANDREW Ay, ay. I care not for good life.

FESTE O mistress mine, where are you roaming? *Sings*
40   O stay and hear, your true love's coming,
      That can sing both high and low.
      Trip no further, pretty sweeting,
      Journeys end in lovers meeting,
      Every wise man's son doth know.

45 SIR ANDREW Excellent good, i'faith.

SIR TOBY Good, good.

FESTE What is love? 'Tis not hereafter, *Sings*
      Present mirth hath present laughter.
      What's to come is still unsure.
50   In delay there lies no plenty,
      Then come kiss me, sweet and twenty,
      Youth's a stuff will not endure.

SIR ANDREW A mellifluous voice, as I am true knight.

SIR TOBY A contagious breath.

55 SIR ANDREW Very sweet and contagious, i'faith.

SIR TOBY To hear by the nose, it is dulcet in contagion.
But shall we make the welkin dance indeed? Shall we
rouse the night owl in a catch that will draw three
souls out of one weaver? Shall we do that?

60 SIR ANDREW An you love me, let's do't. I am dog at a
catch.

FESTE By'r lady, sir, and some dogs will catch well.

SIR ANDREW Most certain. Let our catch be, 'Thou
knave'.

65 FESTE 'Hold thy peace, thou knave', knight? I shall be
constrained in't to call thee knave, knight.

SIR ANDREW 'Tis not the first time I have constrained
one to call me knave. Begin, fool: it begins 'Hold thy
peace'.

70 FESTE I shall never begin if I hold my peace.

SIR ANDREW Good, i'faith. Come, begin. *Catch sung*

41 high and low i.e. in terms of pitch or volume   **42 Trip** go, skip   **sweeting** darling   **47 hereafter** in the future   **49 still** always   **50 plenty** profit   **51 and twenty** an intensifier (the singer's lover is 'twenty times sweet')   **52 stuff** quality/material   **53 true** honest/legitimate   **54 contagious breath** infectious breath/catchy song   **56 hear...nose** i.e. if we inhaled sound   **dulcet in contagion** sweetly contagious
57 welkin sky   **58 rouse** startle/wake   **three souls** three singers would have thrice the effect; powerful music was supposed to draw forth the soul   **59 weaver** often associated with psalm-singing, so to excite one with a drinking song would be a real achievement   **60 dog** i.e. good (Feste plays on the literal sense)   **62 By'r lady** by Our Lady, the Virgin Mary   **63 'Thou knave'** the words of the round
65 Hold thy peace be quiet (subsequent dialogue plays on 'piece', penis)   **66 constrained** compelled

Enter Maria

MARIA What a caterwauling do you keep here? If my
lady have not called up her steward Malvolio and bid
him turn you out of doors, never trust me.

75 SIR TOBY My lady's a Catayan, we are politicians,
Malvolio's a Peg-a-Ramsey, and 'Three merry men
be we'. Am not I consanguineous? Am I not of her
blood? Tillyvally. Lady!

'There dwelt a man in Babylon, lady, lady!'   *Sings*
80 FESTE Beshrew me, the knight's in admirable fooling.

SIR ANDREW Ay, he does well enough if he be disposed,
and so do I too: he does it with a better grace, but I do
it more natural.

SIR TOBY 'O, the twelfth day of December'—   *Sings*
85 MARIA For the love o'God, peace!

Enter Malvolio

MALVOLIO My masters, are you mad? Or what are you?
Have you no wit, manners, nor honesty, but to
gabble like tinkers at this time of night? Do ye make
an alehouse of my lady's house, that ye squeak out
90 your coziers' catches without any mitigation or
remorse of voice? Is there no respect of place,
persons, nor time in you?

SIR TOBY We did keep time, sir, in our catches. Sneck up!

MALVOLIO Sir Toby, I must be round with you. My lady
95 bade me tell you that though she harbours you as
her kinsman, she's nothing allied to your disorders. If
you can separate yourself and your misdemeanours,
you are welcome to the house. If not, an it would
please you to take leave of her, she is very willing to
100 bid you farewell.

SIR TOBY 'Farewell, dear heart, since I must needs be   *Sings*
gone.'

MARIA Nay, good Sir Toby.

---

72 **keep** make   73 **steward** manager of household affairs   75 **Catayan** Catharan (puritan)   **politicians**
schemers   76 **Peg-a-Ramsey** spying wife in a popular ballad   **'Three…we'** popular refrain from a
song   77 **consanguineous** blood-related   78 **Tillyvally** nonsense   79 **'There…lady!'** the opening and
refrain of a song about the biblical tale of Susanna and the Elders   80 **Beshrew** curse   82 **grace**
charm   83 **natural** convincingly/idiotically   84 **'O…December'** from an unidentified song, possibly an
erroneous reference to the twelfth day of Christmas (i.e. Twelfth Night)   87 **wit** good sense   **honesty**
decorum   88 **tinkers** popularly viewed as drunkards   89 **squeak out** i.e. sing shrilly   90 **coziers'**
cobblers'   **mitigation or remorse** considerate lowering   93 **Sneck up!** Shut up!/Buzz off!   94 **round**
blunt   95 **harbours** lodges   96 **nothing allied** not related to   101 **'Farewell…gone'** over the next few
lines Sir Toby and Feste adapt lines from a contemporary ballad

FESTE 'His eyes do show his days are almost done.'		*Sings*
MALVOLIO Is't even so?		

105 **SIR TOBY** 'But I will never die.'   *Sings*

FESTE Sir Toby, there you lie.

MALVOLIO This is much credit to you.

SIR TOBY 'Shall I bid him go?'   *Sings*

FESTE 'What an if you do?'   *Sings*

110 **SIR TOBY** 'Shall I bid him go, and spare not?'   *Sings*

FESTE   'O no, no, no, no, you dare not.'   *Sings*

SIR TOBY Out o'tune, sir, ye lie. Art any more than a
steward? Dost thou think, because thou art virtuous,
there shall be no more cakes and ale?

115 **FESTE** Yes, by Saint Anne, and ginger shall be hot
i'th'mouth too.

SIR TOBY Thou'rt i'th'right. Go, sir, rub your chain with
crumbs. A stoup of wine, Maria!

MALVOLIO Mistress Mary, if you prized my lady's favour
120 at anything more than contempt, you would not give
means for this uncivil rule; she shall know of it, by
this hand.   *Exit*

MARIA Go shake your ears.

SIR ANDREW 'Twere as good a deed as to drink when a
125 man's a-hungry, to challenge him the field, and then
to break promise with him and make a fool of him.

SIR TOBY Do't, knight. I'll write thee a challenge, or I'll
deliver thy indignation to him by word of mouth.

MARIA Sweet Sir Toby, be patient for tonight. Since the
130 youth of the count's was today with my lady, she is
much out of quiet. For Monsieur Malvolio, let me
alone with him: if I do not gull him into a nayword
and make him a common recreation, do not think I
have wit enough to lie straight in my bed. I know I
135 can do it.

SIR TOBY Possess us, possess us, tell us something of
him.

---

104 **Is't even so?** Is that the way things are?   109 **an if** if   110 **spare not** spare him not/be
merciless   112 **Out o' tune** false   **Art** are (you)   114 **cakes and ale** i.e. festivity, particularly abhorrent to
one with puritan tendencies   115 **Saint Anne** mother of the Virgin Mary; another anti-puritan dig   **ginger**
spice in ale/aphrodisiac   117 **rub . . . crumbs** polish your chain of office (reminding Malvolio of his servant
status)   119 **prized** valued   120 **contempt** disrespect/disobedience   **give means** i.e. provide drink
121 **rule** behaviour   123 **Go . . . ears** i.e. like an ass; a dismissive insult   125 **a-hungry** (very) hungry
the field to a duel   131 **out of quiet** agitated   **For** as for   **let . . . him** leave him to me   132 **gull** trick
nayword byword (for stupidity)   133 **recreation** source of amusement   136 **Possess** inform

MARIA Marry, sir, sometimes he is a kind of puritan.

SIR ANDREW O, if I thought that, I'd beat him like a dog!

140 SIR TOBY What, for being a puritan? Thy exquisite reason, dear knight?

SIR ANDREW I have no exquisite reason for't, but I have reason good enough.

MARIA The devil a puritan that he is, or anything
145 constantly, but a time-pleaser, an affectioned ass, that cons state without book and utters it by great swarths. The best persuaded of himself, so crammed, as he thinks, with excellencies, that it is his grounds of faith that all that look on him love him. And on
150 that vice in him will my revenge find notable cause to work.

SIR TOBY What wilt thou do?

MARIA I will drop in his way some obscure epistles of love, wherein, by the colour of his beard, the shape of
155 his leg, the manner of his gait, the expressure of his eye, forehead, and complexion, he shall find himself most feelingly personated. I can write very like my lady your niece: on a forgotten matter we can hardly make distinction of our hands.

160 SIR TOBY Excellent! I smell a device.

SIR ANDREW I have't in my nose too.

SIR TOBY He shall think, by the letters that thou wilt drop, that they come from my niece and that she's in love with him.

165 MARIA My purpose is, indeed, a horse of that colour.

SIR ANDREW And your horse now would make him an ass.

MARIA Ass, I doubt not.

SIR ANDREW O, 'twill be admirable!

170 MARIA Sport royal, I warrant you. I know my physic will work with him. I will plant you two, and let the fool make a third, where he shall find the letter. Observe

---

138 puritan overly strict moralist; not necessarily a member of the extreme Protestant religious movement   **140 exquisite** ingenious/excellent   **145 constantly** consistently   **time-pleaser** time-server, flatterer   **affectioned** pretentious   **146 cons...book** learns high-flown expressions by heart   **by great swarths** in broad sweeps (like quantities of scythed hay)   **147 The best persuaded** having the highest opinion   **148 excellencies** excellent features/accomplishments   **grounds of faith** foundations of belief   **153 obscure epistles** ambiguous letters   **155 expressure** expression   **156 complexion** appearance/colouring/temperament   **157 feelingly personated** accurately represented   **158 on...matter** when we have forgotten the circumstances in which something was written or what it was about   **159 make distinction of** distinguish between   **hands** handwriting   **160 device** plot   **168 Ass** puns on 'as'   **170 physic** medicine/treatment

       his construction of it. For this night, to bed, and
       dream on the event. Farewell.   *Exit*

175   SIR TOBY Good night, Penthesilea.

      SIR ANDREW Before me, she's a good wench.

      SIR TOBY She's a beagle, true-bred, and one that adores
       me. What o'that?

      SIR ANDREW I was adored once too.

180   SIR TOBY Let's to bed, knight. Thou hadst need send for
       more money.

      SIR ANDREW If I cannot recover your niece, I am a foul
       way out.

      SIR TOBY Send for money, knight. If thou hast her not

185   i'th'end, call me cut.

      SIR ANDREW If I do not, never trust me, take it how you
       will.

      SIR TOBY Come, come, I'll go burn some sack. 'Tis too
       late to go to bed now. Come, knight, come, knight.

                             Exeunt

Act 2 Scene 4   *running scene 9*

Enter Duke [Orsino], Viola, Curio and others

      ORSINO Give me some music.— Now, good morrow,
       friends.
       Now, good Cesario, but that piece of song,
       That old and antique song we heard last night;
       Methought it did relieve my passion much,

5   More than light airs and recollected terms
       Of these most brisk and giddy-pacèd times.
       Come, but one verse.

      CURIO He is not here, so please your lordship, that
       should sing it.

10   ORSINO Who was it?

      CURIO Feste, the jester, my lord; a fool that the lady
       Olivia's father took much delight in. He is about the
       house.

      ORSINO Seek him out, and play the tune the while.

                         [Exit Curio]

---

173 **construction** interpretation   174 **event** outcome   175 **Penthesilea** Queen of the Amazons; probably refers to Maria's shortness   176 **Before me** mild oath like 'upon my soul'   177 **beagle** skilful hunting dog   182 **recover** obtain/win   **foul way out** miserably far from success/badly out of pocket   185 **cut** carthorse (castrated or with docked tail)/vagina   188 **burn** warm/sweeten with burnt sugar   **sack** Spanish white wine   **2.4**   2 **but** (I want to hear) only   3 **antique** quaint/old   4 **passion** suffering   5 **airs** melodies   **recollected terms** studied, artificial expressions   14 **the while** in the meantime

15 Come hither, boy. If ever thou shalt love, *Music plays*
     In the sweet pangs of it remember me,
     For such as I am, all true lovers are:
     Unstaid and skittish in all motions else,
     Save in the constant image of the creature
20   That is beloved. How dost thou like this tune?
VIOLA It gives a very echo to the seat
     Where love is throned.
ORSINO Thou dost speak masterly.
     My life upon't, young though thou art, thine eye
25   Hath stayed upon some favour that it loves:
     Hath it not, boy?
VIOLA A little, by your favour.
ORSINO What kind of woman is't?
VIOLA Of your complexion.
30 **ORSINO** She is not worth thee, then. What years, i'faith?
VIOLA About your years, my lord.
ORSINO Too old by heaven. Let still the woman take
     An elder than herself, so wears she to him,
     So sways she level in her husband's heart.
35   For, boy, however we do praise ourselves,
     Our fancies are more giddy and unfirm,
     More longing, wavering, sooner lost and worn,
     Than women's are.
VIOLA I think it well, my lord.
40 **ORSINO** Then let thy love be younger than thyself,
     Or thy affection cannot hold the bent,
     For women are as roses, whose fair flower
     Being once displayed, doth fall that very hour.
VIOLA And so they are. Alas, that they are so.
45   To die, even when they to perfection grow!
Enter Curio and Clown [Feste]
ORSINO O, fellow, come, the song we had last night.—   *To Feste*
     Mark it, Cesario, it is old and plain;
     The spinsters and the knitters in the sun
     And the free maids that weave their thread with
       bones

18 **Unstaid and skittish** unsettled and fickle   **motions else** other emotions   19 **constant** faithful
(contemplation of the)   21 **gives . . . throned** reflects the heart exactly   23 **masterly** from experience/
knowingly   25 **stayed** lingered   **favour** face   27 **by your favour** if you please (plays on the sense of 'on
your face')   32 **still** always   33 **wears she** she adapts herself   34 **sways she level** swings in perfect
balance/exerts constant influence   36 **fancies** infatuations   37 **worn** exhausted   39 **I . . . well** I believe it
41 **hold the bent** hold steady (from archery: holding the bow taught)   43 **displayed** unfurled, in full
bloom   47 **Mark** take note of   48 **spinsters** spinners   49 **free** carefree/innocent   **weave . . . bones** make
lace with bone bobbins

50   Do use to chant it. It is silly sooth,
      And dallies with the innocence of love,
      Like the old age.

FESTE Are you ready, sir?

ORSINO I prithee sing.   *Music*

FESTE   *The song*

55   Come away, come away, death,   *Sings*
            And in sad cypress let me be laid.
            Fly away, fly away, breath,
            I am slain by a fair cruel maid.
            My shroud of white, stuck all with yew,
60   O, prepare it!
            My part of death, no one so true
            Did share it.

            Not a flower, not a flower, sweet
            On my black coffin let there be strewn.
65   Not a friend, not a friend greet
            My poor corpse, where my bones shall be
                thrown.
            A thousand thousand sighs to save,
            Lay me, O, where
            Sad true lover never find my grave,
70   To weep there!

ORSINO There's for thy pains.

FESTE No pains, sir. I take pleasure in singing, sir.

ORSINO I'll pay thy pleasure then.

FESTE Truly, sir, and pleasure will be paid, one time or
75   another.

ORSINO Give me now leave to leave thee.

FESTE Now, the melancholy god protect thee, and the
      tailor make thy doublet of changeable taffeta, for thy
      mind is a very opal. I would have men of such
80   constancy put to sea, that their business might be
      everything and their intent everywhere, for that's it
      that always makes a good voyage of nothing.
      Farewell.   *Exit*

---

50 **Do use** are accustomed   **silly sooth** simple truth   51 **dallies** deals lightly/toys   52 **old age** bygone times, good old days   55 **away** here   56 **cypress** cypress-wood coffin/among sprigs of cypress (associated with mourning)   59 **stuck** adorned, strewn   **yew** yew twigs, also emblematic of mourning   61 **My...it** I am the truest lover who ever died for love   64 **strewn** pronounced 'strown'   74 **pleasure...paid** paid with pain (proverbial)   76 **leave to leave** permission to dismiss   77 **melancholy god** Saturn, thought to govern melancholy dispositions   78 **doublet** close-fitting jacket   **changeable taffeta** shot silk, the colour of which changes depending on the light   79 **opal** iridescent gem of changeable colour   **men...constancy** i.e. inconstant men   80 **their...everywhere** 'he that is everywhere is nowhere' (proverbial)   81 **that's... nothing** that's the attitude that considers a useless voyage to be profitable

ORSINO Let all the rest give place.   *Curio and Attendants stand aside*
                                           Once more, Cesario,
85   Get thee to yond same sovereign cruelty:
        Tell her my love, more noble than the world,
        Prizes not quantity of dirty lands.
        The parts that fortune hath bestowed upon her
        Tell her, I hold as giddily as fortune.
90   But 'tis that miracle and queen of gems
        That nature pranks her in attracts my soul.
VIOLA But if she cannot love you, sir?
ORSINO I cannot be so answered.
VIOLA Sooth, but you must.
95   Say that some lady, as perhaps there is,
        Hath for your love as great a pang of heart
        As you have for Olivia: you cannot love her.
        You tell her so. Must she not then be answered?
ORSINO There is no woman's sides
100   Can bide the beating of so strong a passion
        As love doth give my heart, no woman's heart
        So big, to hold so much. They lack retention.
        Alas, their love may be called appetite,
        No motion of the liver, but the palate,
105   That suffer surfeit, cloyment and revolt.
        But mine is all as hungry as the sea,
        And can digest as much. Make no compare
        Between that love a woman can bear me
        And that I owe Olivia.
110 **VIOLA** Ay, but I know—
ORSINO What dost thou know?
VIOLA Too well what love women to men may owe:
        In faith, they are as true of heart as we.
        My father had a daughter loved a man,
115   As it might be, perhaps, were I a woman,
        I should your lordship.
ORSINO And what's her history?
VIOLA A blank, my lord. She never told her love,
        But let concealment, like a worm i'th'bud,

---

84 give place leave   **87 dirty** dishonourably acquired/despicable/muddy   **88 parts** attributes, i.e. wealth   **89 giddily** lightly   **fortune** traditionally held to be fickle   **90 miracle ... gems** i.e. Olivia's beauty   **91 pranks** adorns   **98 be answered** satisfied   **100 bide** withstand   **102 retention** the power to retain (emotion)   **103 appetite** desire/fancy   **104 motion** impulse/emotion   **liver** thought to be the seat of strong passion   **palate** organ of taste, i.e. easily satisfied   **105 suffer** undergo   **surfeit** sickening over-indulgence   **cloyment** excessive gratification   **revolt** revulsion (of appetite)   **106 mine** i.e. my love **107 compare** comparison   **109 owe** have for   **117 history** story

120   Feed on her damask cheek: she pined in thought,
           And with a green and yellow melancholy
           She sat like patience on a monument,
           Smiling at grief. Was not this love indeed?
           We men may say more, swear more, but indeed
125   Our shows are more than will, for still we prove
           Much in our vows, but little in our love.
           ORSINO But died thy sister of her love, my boy?
           VIOLA I am all the daughters of my father's house,
           And all the brothers too, and yet I know not.
130   Sir, shall I to this lady?
           ORSINO Ay, that's the theme.
           To her in haste: give her this jewel: say   *Gives a jewel*
           My love can give no place, bide no denay.   *Exeunt*

Act 2 Scene 5   *running scene 10*

           Enter Sir Toby, Sir Andrew and Fabian

           SIR TOBY Come thy ways, Signior Fabian.
           FABIAN Nay, I'll come. If I lose a scruple of this sport, let
           me be boiled to death with melancholy.
           SIR TOBY Wouldst thou not be glad to have the
5   niggardly rascally sheep-biter come by some
           notable shame?
           FABIAN I would exult, man. You know he brought me
           out o'favour with my lady about a bear-baiting here.
           SIR TOBY To anger him we'll have the bear again, and
10   we will fool him black and blue. Shall we not, Sir
           Andrew?
           SIR ANDREW An we do not, it is pity of our lives.
           Enter Maria
           SIR TOBY Here comes the little villain.— How now, my   *To Maria*
           metal of India?
15   MARIA Get ye all three into the box-tree: Malvolio's
           coming down this walk. He has been yonder i'the sun
           practising behaviour to his own shadow this half

120 **damask** pink, like the damask rose   121 **green and yellow** sickly, pale and sallow
122 **patience...monument** carved figure on a memorial   125 **shows** outwards displays   **are more** have
more substance   **will** our desires   **still** always   130 **to** go to   133 **give no place** not give way   **denay**
denial   2.5   1 **Come thy ways** come along   2 **scruple** tiny amount   3 **boiled** puns on (black) 'bile', the
cause of **melancholy**; also a joke, since **melancholy** was a cold, dry humour   5 **niggardly** mean-minded
sheep-biter nasty, shifty fellow (literally, a dog that attacks sheep)   8 **bear-baiting** a pastime that was
particularly disapproved of by puritans   10 **fool...blue** bruise him (metaphorically) with fooling
12 **pity...lives** a pity we should live   14 **metal of India** i.e. pure gold, treasure   15 **box-tree** thick
evergreen shrub used in ornamental gardens   16 **walk** path   17 **behaviour** courtly gestures

hour. Observe him, for the love of mockery, for I
know this letter will make a contemplative idiot of
20 him. Close, in the name of jesting! Lie thou there, for   *They hide*
here comes the trout that must be caught with
tickling.   *Puts a letter on the ground*
                                                              Exit

Enter Malvolio   ↓*Sir Toby and the others are not heard by Malvolio*↓

MALVOLIO 'Tis but fortune, all is fortune. Maria once told
me she did affect me, and I have heard herself come
25 thus near, that should she fancy, it should be one of
my complexion. Besides, she uses me with a more
exalted respect than anyone else that follows her.
What should I think on't?

SIR TOBY Here's an overweening rogue!

30 **FABIAN** O, peace! Contemplation makes a rare turkey-
cock of him. How he jets under his advanced plumes!

SIR ANDREW 'Slight, I could so beat the rogue!

SIR TOBY Peace, I say.

MALVOLIO To be Count Malvolio!

35 **SIR TOBY** Ah, rogue!

SIR ANDREW Pistol him, pistol him.

SIR TOBY Peace, peace!

MALVOLIO There is example for't: the lady of the Strachy
married the yeoman of the wardrobe.

40 **SIR ANDREW** Fie on him, Jezebel!

FABIAN O, peace! Now he's deeply in: look how
imagination blows him.

MALVOLIO Having been three months married to her,
sitting in my state—

45 **SIR TOBY** O, for a stone-bow to hit him in the eye!

MALVOLIO Calling my officers about me, in my branched
velvet gown, having come from a daybed, where I
have left Olivia sleeping—

SIR TOBY Fire and brimstone!

---

19 contemplative preoccupied/mindlessly gazing   **20 Close** stay hidden   **22 tickling** i.e. flattery; one
method of catching **trout** is to stroke them under their gills   **24 she** Olivia   **affect** love/feel fondness
for   **25 thus near** i.e. close to saying   **fancy** love   **26 uses** treats   **27 follows** serves   **29 overweening**
arrogant/overambitious   **30 rare** splendid   **turkey-cock** a proverbially proud, vain bird   **31 jets** struts
advanced plumes raised feathers   **32 'Slight** (by) God's light   **36 Pistol** shoot   **38 example** precedent
lady ... wardrobe unknown allusion to the marriage of a woman to her social inferior   **39 yeoman ...
wardrobe** servant in charge of household clothes and linen   **40 Jezebel** in the Bible, proud wife of Ahab,
King of Israel; term for a wicked, deceptive or lascivious woman   **41 in** absorbed in his own fantasies
42 blows him puffs him up   **44 state** canopied chair of state   **45 stone-bow** crossbow that shoots
stones   **46 officers** household servants   **branched** embroidered with a branched pattern or with images of
foliage   **47 daybed** sofa/bed for daytime reclining (with sexual associations)

50 FABIAN O, peace, peace!

    MALVOLIO And then to have the humour of state, and
        after a demure travel of regard, telling them I know
        my place as I would they should do theirs, to ask for
        my kinsman Toby—

55 SIR TOBY Bolts and shackles!

    FABIAN O peace, peace, peace! Now, now.

    MALVOLIO Seven of my people, with an obedient start,
        make out for him. I frown the while, and perchance
        wind up my watch, or play with my— some rich
60   jewel. Toby approaches; curtsies there to me—

    SIR TOBY Shall this fellow live?

    FABIAN Though our silence be drawn from us with cars,
        yet peace.

    MALVOLIO I extend my hand to him thus, quenching my
65   familiar smile with an austere regard of control—

    SIR TOBY And does not Toby take you a blow o'the lips
        then?

    MALVOLIO Saying, 'Cousin Toby, my fortunes having
        cast me on your niece give me this prerogative of
70   speech'—

    SIR TOBY What, what?

    MALVOLIO 'You must amend your drunkenness.'

    SIR TOBY Out, scab!

    FABIAN Nay, patience, or we break the sinews of our plot.

75 MALVOLIO 'Besides, you waste the treasure of your time
        with a foolish knight'—

    SIR ANDREW That's me, I warrant you.

    MALVOLIO 'One Sir Andrew'—

    SIR ANDREW I knew 'twas I, for many do call me fool.

80 MALVOLIO What employment have we here?   *Picks up the letter*

    FABIAN Now is the woodcock near the gin.

    SIR TOBY O, peace! And the spirit of humours intimate
        reading aloud to him.

---

51 **humour of state** temperament/power of one in authority   52 **demure . . . regard** solemn survey of the room and company   53 **would** wish   54 **Toby** Malvolio omits 'Sir'   55 **Bolts and shackles!** restraints for a prisoner   57 **people** servants   **start** sudden movement   58 **make out** go   **perchance** perhaps   59 **my—** perhaps chain of office, which Malvolio momentarily forgets he would not be wearing, but he could be referring to anything; a genital quibble is probably present   60 **curtsies** bows   62 **cars** chariots/carts, i. e. by torture   65 **familiar** friendly   **regard of control** authoritative look   66 **take** strike, give   68 **Cousin** kinsman   69 **prerogative** due privilege, right   73 **scab** scoundrel   74 **sinews** muscles, strength   80 **employment** business   81 **woodcock** proverbially stupid bird   **gin** trap   82 **humours** whims, moods   **intimate** suggest

MALVOLIO By my life, this is my lady's hand these be her
85   very C's, her U's and her T's, and thus makes she her
        great P's. It is in contempt of question her hand.

SIR ANDREW Her C's, her U's and her T's. Why that?

MALVOLIO 'To the unknown beloved, this, and my good   *Reads*
        wishes.' Her very phrases! By your leave, wax. Soft!
90   And the impressure her Lucrece, with which she uses
        to seal. 'Tis my lady. To whom should this be?

FABIAN This wins him, liver and all.

MALVOLIO 'Jove knows I love,   *Reads*
                But who?
95   Lips, do not move.
                No man must know.'
        'No man must know.' What follows? The numbers
        altered! 'No man must know.' If this should be thee,
        Malvolio?

100   **SIR TOBY** Marry, hang thee, brock!

MALVOLIO 'I may command where I adore,   *Reads*
                But silence, like a Lucrece knife,
                With bloodless stroke my heart doth gore:
                M.O.A.I. doth sway my life.'

105   **FABIAN** A fustian riddle!

SIR TOBY Excellent wench, say I.

MALVOLIO 'M.O.A.I. doth sway my life.' Nay, but first let
        me see, let me see, let me see.

FABIAN What dish o'poison has she dressed him.

110   **SIR TOBY** And with what wing the staniel checks at it!

MALVOLIO 'I may command where I adore.' Why, she
        may command me! I serve her, she is my lady. Why,
        this is evident to any formal capacity. There is no
        obstruction in this. And the end — what should that
115   alphabetical position portend? If I could make that
        resemble something in me. Softly: M.O.A.I.—

SIR TOBY O, ay, make up that. He is now at a cold scent.

---

84 hand handwriting   **85 C's ... T's** 'cut' was slang for 'vagina', but the joke may well be on 'cunt' (with
and as 'n')   **86 great P's** uppercase P's/noble vagina ('piece')/copious urination   **in contempt of**
beyond   **90 impressure** imprint, seal   **Lucrece** Olivia's seal-ring bears the image of Lucrece, Roman
heroine who committed suicide after being raped   **uses to seal** customarily seals   **92 liver** seat of
passion   **97 numbers altered** metre changed   **100 brock** badger, used contemptuously   **102 Lucrece
knife** knife Lucrece used to kill herself   **104 sway** rule   **105 fustian** nonsensical/pompous (literally, inferior
cloth)   **109 What** what a   **dressed** prepared for   **110 wing** flight/speed   **staniel** kestrel, or small
falcon   **checks** swoops   **113 formal capacity** normal intelligence   **114 obstruction** obstacle
115 position arrangement   **portend** mean   **117 O, ay** puns on the O ... I of M.O.A.I.   **make up** work
out   **at ... scent** has lost the trail

FABIAN Sowter will cry upon't for all this, though it be as
rank as a fox.

120 **MALVOLIO** M. — Malvolio. M. — Why, that begins my
name!

FABIAN Did not I say he would work it out? The cur is
excellent at faults.

MALVOLIO M. — But then there is no consonancy in the
125 sequel that suffers under probation: 'A' should follow
but 'O' does.

FABIAN And O shall end, I hope.

SIR TOBY Ay, or I'll cudgel him, and make him cry O!

MALVOLIO And then I comes behind.

130 **FABIAN** Ay, an you had any eye behind you, you might
see more detraction at your heels than fortunes
before you.

MALVOLIO M.O.A.I. This simulation is not as the former.
And yet, to crush this a little, it would bow to me, for   *Reads*
135 every one of these letters are in my name. Soft, here
follows prose: 'If this fall into thy hand, revolve. In
my stars I am above thee, but be not afraid of
greatness: some are born great, some achieve
greatness, and some have greatness thrust upon
140 'em. Thy Fates open their hands. Let thy blood and
spirit embrace them. And to inure thyself to what
thou art like to be, cast thy humble slough and
appear fresh. Be opposite with a kinsman, surly with
servants. Let thy tongue tang arguments of state; put
145 thyself into the trick of singularity. She thus advises
thee that sighs for thee. Remember who commended
thy yellow stockings, and wished to see thee ever
cross-gartered. I say, remember. Go to, thou art
made, if thou desirest to be so. If not, let me see thee a
150 steward still, the fellow of servants, and not worthy

---

118 Sowter name of a hound (a 'souter' was a cobbler)   **cry** bark   **119 rank** foul-smelling   **122 cur**
dog   **123 faults** finding the scent again after the trail has gone cold   **124 consonancy . . . sequel**
consistency of pattern   **125 suffers** holds up   **probation** investigation   **127 O shall end** O ends
Malvolio's name/a cry of misery will end this business/the hangman's noose ends life   **130 eye** puns on Ay
and **I**   **131 detraction** defamation, slander   **133 simulation** disguised meaning   **former** earlier, clearer
parts of the letter   **134 crush** force a meaning from   **bow** yield   **136 revolve** consider (with play on 'turn
round', which may cue Malvolio to do so)   **137 stars** fortunes   **140 open their hands** offer bounty
blood and spirit i.e. all of you, body and soul   **141 embrace** willingly accept   **inure** accustom   **142 like**
likely   **cast** cast off   **slough** outer skin   **143 opposite** antagonistic/contradictory   **144 tang . . . state**
ring out on political topics   **145 trick of singularity** peculiar, distinctive behaviour   **147 ever** at all
times   **148 cross-gartered** wearing garters crossed near the knee   **Go to** i.e. come on

to touch Fortune's fingers. Farewell. She that would
alter services with thee,
            The Fortunate-Unhappy.'
Daylight and champaign discovers not more. This is
155 open. I will be proud, I will read politic authors, I will
baffle Sir Toby, I will wash off gross acquaintance, I
will be point-device the very man. I do not now fool
myself, to let imagination jade me; for every reason
excites to this, that my lady loves me. She did
160 commend my yellow stockings of late, she did praise
my leg being cross-gartered. And in this she
manifests herself to my love, and with a kind of
injunction drives me to these habits of her liking. I
thank my stars, I am happy. I will be strange, stout,
165 in yellow stockings, and cross-gartered, even with
the swiftness of putting on. Jove and my stars be
praised! Here is yet a postscript: 'Thou canst not   *Reads*
choose but know who I am. If thou entertainest my
love, let it appear in thy smiling. Thy smiles become
170 thee well: therefore in my presence still smile, dear
my sweet, I prithee.' Jove, I thank thee. I will smile. I
will do everything that thou wilt have me.   *Exit*

Sir Toby, Sir Andrew and Fabian come out of hiding

FABIAN I will not give my part of this sport for a pension
of thousands to be paid from the Sophy.
175 **SIR TOBY** I could marry this wench for this device.
SIR ANDREW So could I too.
SIR TOBY And ask no other dowry with her but such
another jest.
Enter Maria
SIR ANDREW Nor I neither.
180 **FABIAN** Here comes my noble gull-catcher.
SIR TOBY Wilt thou set thy foot o'my neck?
SIR ANDREW Or o'mine either?
SIR TOBY Shall I play my freedom at tray-trip, and
become thy bondslave?

---

152 alter services exchange places of mistress and servant; with sexual innuendo   **153 Fortunate-
Unhappy** i.e. wealthy, but lacking requited love   **154 champaign** open countryside   **discovers**
reveals   **155 open** clear   **politic** political/prudent   **156 baffle** publicly disgrace   **gross** dull/base
157 point-device to the last detail   **158 jade** deceive   **159 excites** urges   **162 manifests herself to**
reveals herself as   **163 injunction** order   **habits** ways of dressing/behaviour   **164 happy** fortunate
strange aloof   **stout** proud, haughty   **168 entertainest** welcome, accept   **170 still** always   **174 Sophy**
Shah of Persia   **175 device** plot   **180 gull-catcher** fool-trapper/trickster   **181 Wilt…neck?** i.e. I submit
totally to you   **183 play** gamble   **tray-trip** type of dicing game   **184 bondslave** slave

185   SIR ANDREW I'faith, or I either?
      SIR TOBY Why, thou hast put him in such a dream that
         when the image of it leaves him, he must run mad.
      MARIA Nay, but say true, does it work upon him?
      SIR TOBY Like aqua-vitae with a midwife.
190   MARIA If you will then see the fruits of the sport, mark
         his first approach before my lady: he will come to her
         in yellow stockings, and 'tis a colour she abhors, and
         cross-gartered, a fashion she detests. And he will
         smile upon her, which will now be so unsuitable to
195   her disposition, being addicted to a melancholy as she
         is, that it cannot but turn him into a notable
         contempt. If you will see it, follow me.
      SIR TOBY To the gates of Tartar, thou most excellent
         devil of wit!
200   SIR ANDREW I'll make one too.   *Exeunt*

Act 3 Scene 1   *running scene 10 continues*

Enter Viola and Clown [Feste, with a tabor]

      VIOLA Save thee, friend, and thy music. Dost thou live by
         thy tabor?
      FESTE No, sir, I live by the church.
      VIOLA Art thou a churchman?
5   FESTE No such matter, sir. I do live by the church, for I
         do live at my house, and my house doth stand by the
         church.
      VIOLA So thou mayst say, the king lies by a beggar, if a
         beggar dwell near him, or the church stands by thy
10   tabor, if thy tabor stand by the church.
      FESTE You have said, sir. To see this age! A sentence is
         but a cheveril glove to a good wit. How quickly the
         wrong side may be turned outward!
      VIOLA Nay, that's certain. They that dally nicely with
15   words may quickly make them wanton.
      FESTE I would, therefore, my sister had had no name, sir.
      VIOLA Why, man?

---

189 **aqua-vitae** strong spirits, such as brandy   190 **fruits** outcome   197 **contempt** object of contempt
198 **Tartar** Tartarus, hell of classical mythology   200 **make one** join in, tag along   3.1 *tabor* small
drum   1 **Save** God save   **live by** earn your living with (Feste plays on the sense of **by** as 'next to')   8 **lies**
by dwells near/sleeps with   9 **stands** is maintained   10 **stand** is placed   11 **You have said** you have had
your say/fair enough   **sentence** saying   12 **cheveril** kidskin (pliable leather)   14 **dally nicely** play
subtly/triflingly   15 **wanton** uncontrolled, ambiguous/lecherous

FESTE Why, sir, her name's a word, and to dally with
that word might make my sister wanton. But indeed,
20   words are very rascals since bonds disgraced them.

VIOLA Thy reason, man?

FESTE Troth, sir, I can yield you none without words,
and words are grown so false, I am loath to prove
reason with them.

25   **VIOLA** I warrant thou art a merry fellow and car'st for
nothing.

FESTE Not so, sir, I do care for something. But in my
conscience, sir, I do not care for you: if that be to care
for nothing, sir, I would it would make you invisible.

30   **VIOLA** Art not thou the lady Olivia's fool?

FESTE No, indeed, sir, the lady Olivia has no folly. She
will keep no fool, sir, till she be married, and fools are
as like husbands as pilchards are to herrings: the
husband's the bigger. I am indeed not her fool, but
35   her corrupter of words.

VIOLA I saw thee late at the count Orsino's.

FESTE Foolery, sir, does walk about the orb like the sun,
it shines everywhere. I would be sorry, sir, but the
fool should be as oft with your master as with my
40   mistress. I think I saw your wisdom there.

VIOLA Nay, an thou pass upon me, I'll no more with
thee. Hold, there's expenses for thee.   *Gives money*

FESTE Now Jove, in his next commodity of hair, send
thee a beard!

45   **VIOLA** By my troth I'll tell thee, I am almost sick for
one— though I would not have it grow on my   *Aside*
chin.— Is thy lady within?

FESTE Would not a pair of these have bred, sir?

VIOLA Yes, being kept together and put to use.

50   **FESTE** I would play Lord Pandarus of Phrygia, sir, to
bring a Cressida to this Troilus.

VIOLA I understand you, sir. 'Tis well begged.   *Gives more money*

FESTE The matter, I hope, is not great, sir; begging but a
beggar. Cressida was a beggar. My lady is within, sir.

---

20 bonds legal contracts   **disgraced them** i.e. by suggesting that a man's word alone was not enough
22 yield give   **33 pilchards** small fish that resemble herring   **36 late** recently   **37 orb** planet, world
38 but were it not for the fact that   **40 your wisdom** i.e. you, a hired servant/fool   **41 pass upon** jest at/
judge   **43 commodity** supply   **45 for one** wanting a beard/from love for a bearded man   **48 these** i.e.
coins   **bred** multiplied; Feste asks for more money   **49 put to use** invested for profit (plays on the sense of
'having had sex')   **50 Pandarus** uncle to Cressida and go-between for his niece and her lover
Troilus   **Phrygia** country in Asia Minor where Troy was situated   **54 Cressida...beggar** in some
versions of the story, Cressida became a beggar with leprosy

55   I will conster to them whence you come. Who you
      are and what you would are out of my welkin. I
      might say 'element', but the word is over-worn. *Exit*
      VIOLA This fellow is wise enough to play the fool,
      And to do that well craves a kind of wit:
60   He must observe their mood on whom he jests,
      The quality of persons, and the time,
      And, like the haggard, check at every feather
      That comes before his eye. This is a practice
      As full of labour as a wise man's art,
65   For folly that he wisely shows is fit;
      But wise men, folly-fall'n, quite taint their wit.
      Enter Sir Toby and Andrew
      SIR TOBY Save you, gentleman.
      VIOLA And you, sir.
      SIR ANDREW *Dieu vous garde, monsieur.*
70   VIOLA *Et vous aussi. Votre serviteur.*
      SIR ANDREW I hope, sir, you are, and I am yours.
      SIR TOBY Will you encounter the house? My niece is
      desirous you should enter, if your trade be to her.
      VIOLA I am bound to your niece, sir. I mean she is the list
75   of my voyage.
      SIR TOBY Taste your legs, sir, put them to motion.
      VIOLA My legs do better understand me, sir, than I
      understand what you mean by bidding me taste my
      legs.
80   SIR TOBY I mean, to go, sir, to enter.
      VIOLA I will answer you with gait and entrance. But we
      are prevented.
      Enter Olivia and Gentlewoman [Maria]
      Most excellent accomplished lady, the heavens rain
      odours on you!
85   SIR ANDREW That youth's a rare courtier. 'Rain odours',   *To Toby*
      well.
      VIOLA My matter hath no voice, lady, but to your own
      most pregnant and vouchsafed ear.

---

55 **conster** explain   56 **out…welkin** beyond me   **welkin** sky, heavens   57 **element** sphere of
knowledge/sky   59 **craves** requires   61 **quality** character/rank   62 **haggard** untrained hawk   **check**
swoop   63 **practice** occupation   65 **is fit** suits the purpose   66 **folly-fall'n** stooping to foolishness
69 *Dieu…monsieur* 'God save you, sir' (French)   70 *Et…serviteur* 'And you, too. [I am] your servant'
(French)   72 **encounter** approach/enter   73 **trade** business, with sexual innuendo   **to** with, concerning
74 **bound to** heading for   **list** limit, objective   76 **Taste** try out   77 **understand** support/comprehend
81 **gait and entrance** corresponding nouns to Sir Toby's verbs; **gait** puns on 'gate'   82 **prevented**
anticipated/forestalled   83 **the** may the   84 **odours** sweet smells   87 **hath no voice** cannot be uttered
88 **pregnant** receptive   **vouchsafed** (kindly) bestowed, i.e. attentive

SIR ANDREW 'Odours,' 'pregnant' and 'vouchsafed'. I'll   *To Toby*
90   get 'em all three all ready.

OLIVIA Let the garden door be shut, and leave me to my
        hearing.—

                    [*Exeunt Sir Toby, Sir Andrew and Maria*]
        Give me your hand, sir.

VIOLA My duty, madam, and most humble service.

95 OLIVIA What is your name?

VIOLA Cesario is your servant's name, fair princess.

OLIVIA My servant, sir? 'Twas never merry world
        Since lowly feigning was called compliment.
        You're servant to the count Orsino, youth.

100 VIOLA And he is yours, and his must needs be yours:
        Your servant's servant is your servant, madam.

OLIVIA For him, I think not on him: for his thoughts,
        Would they were blanks, rather than filled with me!

VIOLA Madam, I come to whet your gentle thoughts
105   On his behalf.

OLIVIA O, by your leave, I pray you.
        I bade you never speak again of him;
        But, would you undertake another suit,
        I had rather hear you to solicit that
110   Than music from the spheres.

VIOLA Dear lady—

OLIVIA Give me leave, beseech you. I did send,
        After the last enchantment you did here,
        A ring in chase of you: so did I abuse
115   Myself, my servant and, I fear me, you.
        Under your hard construction must I sit,
        To force that on you, in a shameful cunning,
        Which you knew none of yours. What might you
            think?
        Have you not set mine honour at the stake
120   And baited it with all th'unmuzzled thoughts
        That tyrannous heart can think? To one of your
            receiving

---

90 all ready committed to memory, ready for use   **92 hearing** audience (with Cesario)   **97 'Twas** . . .
world proverbial: things haven't been the same   **98 lowly feigning** pretended modesty   **compliment**
courtesy   **100 yours** your servant   **his** i.e. his servants   **102 For** as for   **103 blanks** blank paper/
unstamped coins   **108 suit** petition, courtship   **109 solicit** urge   **110 music** . . . **spheres** planets and stars
were thought to be surrounded by hollow spheres that produced beautiful music as they rotated   **112 leave**
permission (to speak)   **114 abuse** wrong/disgrace   **116 construction** judgement/interpretation (of my
conduct)   **117 To force** for forcing   **119 stake** post to which a bear is chained for baiting by dogs
121 receiving understanding

Enough is shown: a cypress, not a bosom,
Hides my heart. So, let me hear you speak.
VIOLA I pity you.
125 **OLIVIA** That's a degree to love.
VIOLA No, not a grize, for 'tis a vulgar proof,
That very oft we pity enemies.
OLIVIA Why, then, methinks 'tis time to smile again.
O, world, how apt the poor are to be proud!
130 If one should be a prey, how much the better
To fall before the lion than the wolf!   *Clock strikes*
The clock upbraids me with the waste of time.
Be not afraid, good youth, I will not have you:
And yet, when wit and youth is come to harvest,
135 Your wife is like to reap a proper man.
There lies your way, due west.
VIOLA Then westward-ho! Grace and good disposition
Attend your ladyship!
You'll nothing, madam, to my lord by me?
140 **OLIVIA** Stay.
I prithee tell me what thou think'st of me.
VIOLA That you do think you are not what you are.
OLIVIA If I think so, I think the same of you.
VIOLA Then think you right: I am not what I am.
145 **OLIVIA** I would you were as I would have you be.
VIOLA Would it be better, madam, than I am?
I wish it might, for now I am your fool.
OLIVIA O, what a deal of scorn looks beautiful
In the contempt and anger of his lip!
150 A murd'rous guilt shows not itself more soon
Than love that would seem hid: love's night is noon.
Cesario, by the roses of the spring,
By maidhood, honour, truth and everything,
I love thee so that, maugre all thy pride,
155 Nor wit nor reason can my passion hide.
Do not extort thy reasons from this clause,
For that I woo, thou therefore hast no cause,

---

122 cypress light transparent material   **125 degree** step   **126 grize** step   **vulgar proof** common
experience   **128 smile again** i.e. throw off melancholy   **131 lion** a more noble adversary   **135 proper**
handsome/worthy   **137 disposition** state of mind   **139 You'll** you'll send   **142 what you are** i.e. in love
with me (a woman/a servant)   **147 I...fool** you make me look foolish   **148 deal** quantity
151 love's...noon i.e. despite trying to conceal itself, love is obvious   **153 maidhood** virginity
154 maugre in spite of   **155 Nor** neither   **156 extort...clause** extract reason from this premise
157 For that because   **no cause** need to woo in return

But rather reason thus with reason fetter:
Love sought is good, but given unsought is better.
160 VIOLA By innocence I swear, and by my youth,
I have one heart, one bosom and one truth,
And that no woman has, nor never none
Shall mistress be of it, save I alone.
And so adieu, good madam. Never more
165 Will I my master's tears to you deplore.
OLIVIA Yet come again, for thou perhaps mayst move
That heart which now abhors, to like his love. *Exeunt*

Act 3 Scene 2   *running scene 11*

Enter Sir Toby, Sir Andrew and Fabian

SIR ANDREW No, faith, I'll not stay a jot longer.
SIR TOBY Thy reason, dear venom, give thy reason.
FABIAN You must needs yield your reason, Sir Andrew.
SIR ANDREW Marry, I saw your niece do more favours to
5 the count's servingman than ever she bestowed upon
me. I saw't i'th'orchard.
SIR TOBY Did she see thee the while, old boy? Tell me
that.
SIR ANDREW As plain as I see you now.
10 FABIAN This was a great argument of love in her toward
you.
SIR ANDREW 'Slight, will you make an ass o'me?
FABIAN I will prove it legitimate, sir, upon the oaths of
judgement and reason.
15 SIR TOBY And they have been grand-jurymen since
before Noah was a sailor.
FABIAN She did show favour to the youth in your sight
only to exasperate you, to awake your dormouse
valour, to put fire in your heart and brimstone in
20 your liver. You should then have accosted her, and
with some excellent jests, fire-new from the mint,
you should have banged the youth into dumbness.
This was looked for at your hand, and this was
balked. The double gilt of this opportunity you let

---

158 **reason . . . fetter** restrain your reason with the following reasoning   165 **deplore** lament, recount
sorrowfully   3.2   2 **venom** venomous person   6 **i'th'orchard** in the garden   7 **the while** at the time
10 **argument** proof   13 **it** my case   **oaths** sworn testament   16 **Noah** biblical character who survived a
mighty flood sent by God   18 **dormouse** sleepy   21 **fire-new . . . mint** i.e. like a freshly minted coin
22 **banged** struck   24 **balked** avoided/neglected   **double gilt** i.e. golden (**opportunity**)

25   time wash off, and you are now sailed into the north
of my lady's opinion, where you will hang like an
icicle on a Dutchman's beard, unless you do redeem
it by some laudable attempt either of valour or policy.

SIR ANDREW An't be any way, it must be with valour, for
30   policy I hate: I had as lief be a Brownist as a
politician.

SIR TOBY Why, then, build me thy fortunes upon the
basis of valour. Challenge me the count's youth to
fight with him. Hurt him in eleven places: my niece
35   shall take note of it. And assure thyself, there is no
love-broker in the world can more prevail in man's
commendation with woman than report of valour.

FABIAN There is no way but this, Sir Andrew.

SIR ANDREW Will either of you bear me a challenge to
40   him?

SIR TOBY Go, write it in a martial hand. Be curst and
brief: it is no matter how witty, so it be eloquent and
full of invention. Taunt him with the licence of ink. If
thou thou'st him some thrice, it shall not be amiss.
45   And as many lies as will lie in thy sheet of paper,
although the sheet were big enough for the bed of
Ware in England, set 'em down. Go, about it. Let
there be gall enough in thy ink, though thou write
with a goose-pen, no matter. About it.

50   SIR ANDREW Where shall I find you?

SIR TOBY We'll call thee at the *cubiculo*. Go.

                                                    Exit Sir Andrew

FABIAN This is a dear manikin to you, Sir Toby.

SIR TOBY I have been dear to him, lad, some two
thousand strong, or so.

55   FABIAN We shall have a rare letter from him; but you'll
not deliver't?

SIR TOBY Never trust me, then. And by all means stir on
the youth to an answer. I think oxen and wainropes

---

25 north cold region   **28 policy** strategy   **30 lief** willingly   **Brownist** follower of Robert Browne, founder
of an extreme puritan sect   **31 politician** schemer   **32 build me** build   **33 Challenge me** challenge
36 love-broker go-between   **41 martial hand** military style/handwriting   **curst** quarrelsome   **42 so**
provided that   **43 invention** innovation   **licence of ink** freedom encouraged by writing rather than
speaking   **44 thou'st** call him 'thou', an insult to a stranger ('you' is the polite form)   **45 lies** accusations of
lying   **46 bed of Ware** famous bed, able to hold twelve people   **48 gall** bile, anger/an ingredient in ink
(oak-gall)   **49 goose-pen** quill-pen made from a goose's feather (may play on sense of goose as 'fool')
51 *cubiculo* 'bedroom' (Latin)   **52 manikin** little man, puppet   **53 dear** costly   **two thousand** probably
ducats (gold coins)   **55 rare** marvellous, i.e. entertaining   **58 wainropes** wagon ropes, pulled by oxen

cannot hale them together. For Andrew, if he were
60   opened and you find so much blood in his liver as will
clog the foot of a flea, I'll eat the rest of th'anatomy.
FABIAN And his opposite, the youth, bears in his visage
no great presage of cruelty.

Enter Maria

SIR TOBY Look where the youngest wren of mine comes.
65   MARIA If you desire the spleen, and will laugh yourselves
into stitches, follow me. Yond gull Malvolio is turned
heathen, a very renegado; for there is no Christian
that means to be saved by believing rightly can ever
believe such impossible passages of grossness. He's in
70   yellow stockings.

SIR TOBY And cross-gartered?

MARIA Most villainously: like a pedant that keeps a
school i'th'church. I have dogged him like his
murderer. He does obey every point of the letter
75   that I dropped to betray him: he does smile his face
into more lines than is in the new map with the
augmentation of the Indies. You have not seen such
a thing as 'tis. I can hardly forbear hurling things at
him. I know my lady will strike him. If she do, he'll
80   smile and take't for a great favour.

SIR TOBY Come, bring us, bring us where he is. *Exeunt*

Act 3 Scene 3   *running scene 12*

Enter Sebastian and Antonio

SEBASTIAN I would not by my will have troubled you,
But since you make your pleasure of your pains,
I will no further chide you.

ANTONIO I could not stay behind you: my desire,
5   More sharp than filèd steel, did spur me forth,
And not all love to see you, though so much
As might have drawn one to a longer voyage,
But jealousy what might befall your travel,

59 hale haul, drag   61 th'anatomy i.e. his skeleton/body   62 opposite adversary   visage appearance/
face   63 presage indication   64 youngest wren the wren is a small bird (a play on Maria's size); some
editors emend 'mine' to 'nine'   65 spleen fit of laughter (the spleen was thought to be the seat of
laughter)   66 gull fool, dupe   67 renegado deserter of his religion   69 passages of grossness i.e. the
ludicrous statements in Maria's letter   72 villainously offensively, horribly   pedant schoolmaster
73 dogged followed closely   76 new ... Indies probably refers to a map published in 1599 that showed the
East Indies in much greater detail than previously   78 forbear desist from   3.3 3 chide scold   5 filèd
sharpened   6 all only (out of)   so much enough (love)   8 jealousy concern, apprehension (about)

Being skill-less in these parts, which to a stranger,
10 Unguided and unfriended, often prove
Rough and unhospitable. My willing love,
The rather by these arguments of fear,
Set forth in your pursuit.
SEBASTIAN My kind Antonio,
15 I can no other answer make but thanks,
And thanks, and ever oft good turns
Are shuffled off with such uncurrent pay.
But were my worth, as is my conscience, firm,
You should find better dealing. What's to do?
20 Shall we go see the relics of this town?
ANTONIO Tomorrow, sir. Best first go see your lodging.
SEBASTIAN I am not weary, and 'tis long to night.
I pray you let us satisfy our eyes
With the memorials and the things of fame
25 That do renown this city.
ANTONIO Would you'd pardon me.
I do not without danger walk these streets.
Once in a sea-fight gainst the count his galleys
I did some service, of such note indeed,
30 That were I ta'en here it would scarce be answered.
SEBASTIAN Belike you slew great number of his people.
ANTONIO Th'offence is not of such a bloody nature,
Albeit the quality of the time and quarrel
Might well have given us bloody argument.
35 It might have since been answered in repaying
What we took from them, which for traffic's sake,
Most of our city did. Only myself stood out,
For which, if I be lapsèd in this place,
I shall pay dear.
40 SEBASTIAN Do not then walk too open.
ANTONIO It doth not fit me. Hold, sir, here's my purse.   *Gives his purse*
In the south suburbs, at the Elephant,
Is best to lodge. I will bespeak our diet,
Whiles you beguile the time and feed your knowledge

---

9 skill-less in unacquainted with   **stranger** foreigner   **12 rather** more readily   **16 ever oft** very often
17 shuffled off shrugged aside   **uncurrent** worthless   **18 worth** financial means   **conscience** feeling of
obligation   **firm** substantial/reliable   **19 dealing** treatment/reward   **20 relics** antiquities, old sights
25 renown make famous   **28 count his** count's, i.e. duke's   **galleys** ships usually propelled by oars as well
as sails   **30 it . . . answered** it would be virtually impossible to account for it/make reparation (i.e. Antonio's
life would be in danger)   **31 Belike** presumably   **33 Albeit** even though   **34 bloody argument** cause for
shedding blood   **35 answered** requited   **36 traffic's** trade's   **38 lapsèd** apprehended/caught out
40 open publicly   **41 doth not fit** does not suit/is not appropriate for   **42 Elephant** name of an inn
43 bespeak our diet order our food   **44 beguile** while away

45   With viewing of the town. There shall you have me.

SEBASTIAN Why I your purse?

ANTONIO Haply your eye shall light upon some toy
You have desire to purchase, and your store,
I think, is not for idle markets, sir.

50   **SEBASTIAN** I'll be your purse-bearer and leave you
For an hour.

ANTONIO To th'Elephant.

SEBASTIAN I do remember.   *Exeunt*

Act 3 Scene 4   *running scene 13*

Enter Olivia and Maria

OLIVIA I have sent after him: he says he'll come.   *Aside*
How shall I feast him? What bestow of him?
For youth is bought more oft than begged or
      borrowed.
I speak too loud.—

5   Where's Malvolio? He is sad and civil,
And suits well for a servant with my fortunes.
Where is Malvolio?

MARIA He's coming, madam, but in very strange
manner. He is sure possessed, madam.

10   **OLIVIA** Why, what's the matter? Does he rave?

MARIA No, madam, he does nothing but smile: your
ladyship were best to have some guard about you, if
he come, for sure the man is tainted in's wits.

OLIVIA Go call him hither.— I am as mad as he,   *Maria goes to*
15   If sad and merry madness equal be.   *call Malvolio*

Enter Malvolio [cross-gartered and in yellow stockings]
How now, Malvolio?

MALVOLIO Sweet lady, ho, ho.

OLIVIA Smilest thou? I sent for thee upon a sad occasion.

MALVOLIO Sad, lady? I could be sad: this does make some
20   obstruction in the blood, this cross-gartering, but
what of that? If it please the eye of one, it is with me
as the very true sonnet is, 'Please one, and please all'.

OLIVIA Why, how dost thou, man? What is the matter
with thee?

---

45 **have** meet   47 **Haply** perhaps   **toy** trifle   48 **store** available money   49 **idle markets** trivial
purchases   **3.4   1 him** i.e. Cesario   **2 of** on   **5 sad** serious   **civil** decorous   **9 possessed** by evil spirits,
i.e. mad   **19 sad** serious/melancholy   **22 sonnet** song/poem   **'Please … all'** a ballad about women
having their own way sexually

25 MALVOLIO Not black in my mind, though yellow in my
legs. It did come to his hands, and commands shall be
executed. I think we do know the sweet Roman
hand.

OLIVIA Wilt thou go to bed, Malvolio?

30 MALVOLIO To bed? Ay, sweetheart, and I'll come to thee.

OLIVIA God comfort thee! Why dost thou smile so and
kiss thy hand so oft?

MARIA How do you, Malvolio?

MALVOLIO At your request! Yes, nightingales answer
35 daws.

MARIA Why appear you with this ridiculous boldness
before my lady?

MALVOLIO 'Be not afraid of greatness.' 'Twas well writ.

OLIVIA What meanest thou by that, Malvolio?

40 MALVOLIO 'Some are born great'—

OLIVIA Ha?

MALVOLIO 'Some achieve greatness'—

OLIVIA What say'st thou?

MALVOLIO 'And some have greatness thrust upon them.'

45 OLIVIA Heaven restore thee!

MALVOLIO 'Remember who commended thy yellow
stockings'—

OLIVIA Thy yellow stockings?

MALVOLIO 'And wished to see thee cross-gartered.'

50 OLIVIA Cross-gartered?

MALVOLIO 'Go to, thou art made, if thou desirest to be
so'—

OLIVIA Am I made?

MALVOLIO 'If not, let me see thee a servant still.'

55 OLIVIA Why, this is very midsummer madness.
Enter Servant

SERVANT Madam, the young gentleman of the count
Orsino's is returned. I could hardly entreat him back.
He attends your ladyship's pleasure.

OLIVIA I'll come to him.   [*Exit Servant*]
60 Good Maria, let this fellow be looked to. Where's my
cousin Toby? Let some of my people have a special
care of him. I would not have him miscarry for the
half of my dowry.   *Exeunt* [*Olivia and Maria*]

---

25 black melancholic (from an excess of black bile)   **26 It** i.e. the letter   **his** i.e. Malvolio's   **27 Roman**
hand fashionable Italian style of handwriting   **29 go to bed** i.e. to rest (but Malvolio takes this as sexually
suggestive)   **32 kiss thy hand** a fashionable greeting amongst courtiers   **35 daws** jackdaws, birds of the crow
family/fools   **55 midsummer** proverbially the season for madness   **57 hardly** with difficulty   **58 attends**
awaits   **62 miscarry** come to harm

MALVOLIO O, ho! Do you come near me now? No worse
65   man than Sir Toby to look to me! This concurs
directly with the letter: she sends him on purpose
that I may appear stubborn to him, for she incites me
to that in the letter. 'Cast thy humble slough,' says
she, 'be opposite with a kinsman, surly with servants,
70   let thy tongue tang with arguments of state, put
thyself   into   the   trick   of   singularity.'   And
consequently sets down the manner how: as, a sad
face, a reverend carriage, a slow tongue, in the habit
of some sir of note, and so forth. I have limed her, but
75   it is Jove's doing, and Jove make me thankful. And
when she went away now, 'Let this fellow be looked
to.' Fellow? Not Malvolio, nor after my degree, but
fellow. Why, everything adheres together, that no
dram of a scruple, no scruple of a scruple, no
80   obstacle, no incredulous or unsafe circumstance —
What can be said? Nothing that can be can come
between me and the full prospect of my hopes. Well,
Jove, not I, is the doer of this, and he is to be thanked.

Enter Toby, Fabian and Maria

SIR TOBY Which way is he, in the name of sanctity? If all
85   the devils of hell be drawn in little, and Legion
himself possessed him, yet I'll speak to him.

FABIAN Here he is, here he is. How is't with you, sir?
How is't with you, man?

MALVOLIO Go off. I discard you. Let me enjoy my private.
90   Go off.

MARIA Lo, how hollow the fiend speaks within him! Did
not I tell you? Sir Toby, my lady prays you to have a
care of him.

MALVOLIO Ah, ha, does she so?

95 **SIR TOBY** Go to, go to. Peace, peace. We must deal
gently with him. Let me alone.— How do you,
Malvolio? How is't with you? What, man, defy the
devil! Consider, he's an enemy to mankind.

---

64 come near begin to understand/appreciate   **72 consequently** subsequently   **73 reverend carriage**
dignified bearing   **habit** manner/clothing   **74 sir of note** distinguished man   **limed** caught; birdlime was
a sticky substance smeared on branches to trap birds   **77 Fellow** equal   **after my degree** according to my
position   **79 dram** tiny amount   **scruple** small quantity/doubt   **80 incredulous** incredible   **unsafe**
unreliable   **85 drawn in little** gathered in a small space/painted in miniature   **Legion** biblical reference to
a multitude of devils; Sir Toby may mistakenly think it is the name of a specific devil   **89 private** privacy,
with possible play on 'private parts'   **91 Lo** look   **hollow** echoingly   **92 have a** take   **96 Let me alone**
leave him to me

MALVOLIO Do you know what you say?

100 **MARIA** La you, an you speak ill of the devil, how he takes it at heart! Pray God, he be not bewitched!

FABIAN Carry his water to th'wise woman.

MARIA Marry, and it shall be done tomorrow morning, if I live. My lady would not lose him for more than I'll
105   say.

MALVOLIO How now, mistress?

MARIA O Lord!

SIR TOBY Prithee hold thy peace, this is not the way. Do you not see you move him? Let me alone with him.

110 **FABIAN** No way but gentleness, gently, gently. The fiend is rough, and will not be roughly used.

SIR TOBY Why, how now, my bawcock? How dost thou, chuck?

MALVOLIO Sir!

115 **SIR TOBY** Ay, Biddy, come with me. What, man, 'tis not for gravity to play at cherry-pit with Satan. Hang him, foul collier!

MARIA Get him to say his prayers, good Sir Toby, get him to pray.

120 **MALVOLIO** My prayers, minx?

MARIA No, I warrant you he will not hear of godliness.

MALVOLIO Go, hang yourselves all! You are idle shallow things. I am not of your element. You shall know more hereafter.   *Exit*

125 **SIR TOBY** Is't possible?

FABIAN If this were played upon a stage now, I could condemn it as an improbable fiction.

SIR TOBY His very genius hath taken the infection of the device, man.

130 **MARIA** Nay, pursue him now, lest the device take air and taint.

FABIAN Why, we shall make him mad indeed.

MARIA The house will be the quieter.

SIR TOBY Come, we'll have him in a dark room and
135   bound. My niece is already in the belief that he's mad. We may carry it thus, for our pleasure and his

---

100 La look   **102 water** urine, examined for diagnosis   **wise woman** local healer, thought able to cure those bewitched   **109 move** excite/provoke   **112 bawcock** good fellow (from the French *beau coq*, i.e. 'fine bird')   **113 chuck** chick   **115 Biddy** hen   **116 gravity** respectability   **cherry-pit** children's game in which cherry-stones are thrown into a hole   **117 foul collier** dirty coalman, i.e. the devil   **122 idle** worthless/trivial   **123 element** sphere/type   **128 genius** soul/guardian spirit   **130 take ... taint** be spoiled (by exposure to air)   **134 in ... bound** conventional treatment for the insane   **136 carry** manage/maintain

penance, till our very pastime, tired out of breath,
prompt us to have mercy on him, at which time we
will bring the device to the bar and crown thee for a
140   finder of madmen. But see, but see.

Enter Sir Andrew

FABIAN More matter for a May morning.

SIR ANDREW   Here's the challenge, read it. I warrant   *Shows a paper*
there's vinegar and pepper in't.

FABIAN Is't so saucy?

145   SIR ANDREW Ay, is't, I warrant him. Do but read.

SIR TOBY Give me. 'Youth, whatsoever thou art, thou   *Reads*
art but a scurvy fellow.'

FABIAN Good, and valiant.

SIR TOBY 'Wonder not, nor admire not in thy mind,   *Reads*
150   why I do call thee so, for I will show thee no reason
for't.'

FABIAN A good note, that keeps you from the blow of the
law.

SIR TOBY 'Thou comest to the lady Olivia, and in my   *Reads*
155   sight she uses thee kindly. But thou liest in thy
throat, that is not the matter I challenge thee for.'

FABIAN Very brief, and to exceeding good sense— less.   *Aside*

SIR TOBY 'I will waylay thee going home, where if it be   *Reads*
thy chance to kill me'—

160   FABIAN Good.

SIR TOBY 'Thou killest me like a rogue and a villain.'   *Reads*

FABIAN Still you keep o'th'windy side of the law. Good.

SIR TOBY 'Fare thee well, and God have mercy upon one   *Reads*
of our souls! He may have mercy upon mine, but my
165   hope is better, and so look to thyself. Thy friend, as
thou usest him, and thy sworn enemy,
                Andrew Aguecheek.'
If this letter move him not, his legs cannot. I'll
give't him.

170   MARIA You may have very fit occasion for't: he is now in
some commerce with my lady, and will by and by
depart.

---

139 bar open court, i.e. judgement   **140 finder of madmen** juror who formally declared whether a man
was mad   **141 matter** substance/sport   **May morning** i.e. festive time   **142 warrant** assure you/
confirm   **144 saucy** spicy/insolent   **145 warrant** assure   **147 scurvy** worthless/contemptible
149 admire marvel   **152 note** remark   **keeps** protects   **blow...law** legal punishment (for breaching the
peace)   **155 liest...throat** lie outrageously   **162 o'th'windy** on the windward, i.e. safe   **165 hope** i.e.
of success   **as...him** insofar as you treat him as such   **168 move** provoke/set in motion
171 commerce transaction/conversational exchange

SIR TOBY Go, Sir Andrew. Scout me for him at the
corner of the orchard like a bumbaily: so soon as ever
175   thou see'st him, draw, and as thou draw'st swear
horrible, for it comes to pass oft that a terrible oath,
with a swaggering accent sharply twanged off, gives
manhood more approbation than ever proof itself
would have earned him. Away!

180   **SIR ANDREW** Nay, let me alone for swearing.   *Exit*

SIR TOBY Now will not I deliver his letter, for the
behaviour of the young gentleman gives him out to
be of good capacity and breeding. His employment
between his lord and my niece confirms no less:
185   therefore this letter, being so excellently ignorant,
will breed no terror in the youth. He will find it comes
from a clodpole. But, sir, I will deliver his challenge
by word of mouth; set upon Aguecheek a notable
report of valour, and drive the gentleman, as I know
190   his youth will aptly receive it, into a most hideous
opinion of his rage, skill, fury and impetuosity. This
will so fright them both that they will kill one
another by the look, like cockatrices.

Enter Olivia and Viola

FABIAN Here he comes with your niece. Give them way
195   till he take leave, and presently after him.

SIR TOBY I will meditate the while upon some horrid
message for a challenge.

                         [*Exeunt Sir Toby, Fabian and Maria*]

OLIVIA I have said too much unto a heart of stone
And laid mine honour too unchary on't.
200   There's something in me that reproves my fault,
But such a headstrong potent fault it is,
That it but mocks reproof.

VIOLA With the same 'haviour that your passion bears
Goes on my master's griefs.

205   **OLIVIA** Here, wear this jewel for me, 'tis my picture.
Refuse it not. It hath no tongue to vex you.
And I beseech you come again tomorrow.

---

173 **Scout me** keep watch (for me)   174 **bumbaily** bailiff who crept up on the debtor from behind
176 **horrible** terribly/exceedingly   177 **twanged off** uttered ringingly/said with a snide nasal intonation
178 **approbation** credit   **proof** testing out   180 **let me alone** i.e. you can rely on me   183 **capacity**
intelligence   187 **clodpole** idiot   190 **youth** inexperience   **aptly receive** readily believe   **hideous**
terrifying   193 **cockatrices** basilisks, mythical reptiles whose gaze had the power to kill   194 **Give them**
way keep out of their way   195 **presently** immediately   196 **horrid** terrifying   199 **laid** laid down/
exposed   **unchary** carelessly   203 **'haviour...bears** behaviour that characterizes your passion
205 **jewel** piece of jewellery, here a miniature portrait of Olivia

What shall you ask of me that I'll deny,
That honour saved may upon asking give?

210 **VIOLA** Nothing but this: your true love for my master.

OLIVIA How with mine honour may I give him that
Which I have given to you?

VIOLA I will acquit you.

OLIVIA Well, come again tomorrow. Fare thee well.

215 A fiend like thee might bear my soul to hell.   [*Exit*]
Enter Toby and Fabian

SIR TOBY Gentleman, God save thee.

VIOLA And you, sir.

SIR TOBY That defence thou hast, betake thee to't. Of
what nature the wrongs are thou hast done him, I

220 know not, but thy intercepter, full of despite, bloody
as the hunter, attends thee at the orchard-end.
Dismount thy tuck, be yare in thy preparation, for
thy assailant is quick, skilful and deadly.

VIOLA You mistake, sir, I am sure. No man hath any

225 quarrel to me: my remembrance is very free and clear
from any image of offence done to any man.

SIR TOBY You'll find it otherwise, I assure you: therefore,
if you hold your life at any price, betake you to your
guard, for your opposite hath in him what youth,

230 strength, skill and wrath can furnish man withal.

VIOLA I pray you, sir, what is he?

SIR TOBY He is knight, dubbed with unhatched rapier
and on carpet consideration, but he is a devil in
private brawl. Souls and bodies hath he divorced

235 three, and his incensement at this moment is so
implacable that satisfaction can be none but by pangs
of death and sepulchre. Hob, nob, is his word: give't
or take't.

VIOLA I will return again into the house and desire some

240 conduct of the lady. I am no fighter. I have heard of
some kind of men that put quarrels purposely on
others, to taste their valour. Belike this is a man of
that quirk.

---

209 honour saved i.e. apart from my virginity   **213 acquit** excuse, release (from obligation to love)
218 That whatever   **betake** resort   **220 intercepter** one lying in wait   **despite** contempt   **bloody**
bloodthirsty   **222 Dismount** draw   **tuck** sword   **yare** quick   **225 to** with   **remembrance** memory
228 price value   **229 opposite** opponent   **230 withal** with   **232 dubbed** invested with knightly
status   **unhatched** unhacked, unmarked (in battle)   **233 on carpet consideration** for courtly, rather
than military, reasons   **235 incensement** fury   **236 satisfaction** recompense for offence to one's
honour   **237 sepulchre** tomb   **Hob, nob** have or have not, i.e. come what may   **word** motto
240 conduct protection   **242 taste** test   **243 quirk** peculiarity

SIR TOBY Sir, no. His indignation derives itself out of a
245   very competent injury: therefore, get you on and give
him his desire. Back you shall not to the house,
unless you undertake that with me which with as
much safety you might answer him: therefore, on, or
strip your sword stark naked, for meddle you must,
250   that's certain, or forswear to wear iron about you.

VIOLA This is as uncivil as strange. I beseech you do me
this courteous office, as to know of the knight what
my offence to him is. It is something of my
negligence, nothing of my purpose.

255 **SIR TOBY** I will do so. Signior Fabian, stay you by this
gentleman till my return.   *Exit Toby*

VIOLA Pray you, sir, do you know of this matter?

FABIAN I know the knight is incensed against you, even
to a mortal arbitrement, but nothing of the
260   circumstance more.

VIOLA I beseech you what manner of man is he?

FABIAN Nothing of that wonderful promise, to read him
by his form, as you are like to find him in the proof of
his valour. He is, indeed, sir, the most skilful, bloody
265   and fatal opposite that you could possibly have found
in any part of Illyria. Will you walk towards him? I
will make your peace with him if I can.

VIOLA I shall be much bound to you for't: I am one that
had rather go with sir priest than sir knight. I care
270   not who knows so much of my mettle.   *Exeunt*

Enter Toby and Andrew

SIR TOBY Why, man, he's a very devil. I have not seen
such a firago. I had a pass with him, rapier, scabbard
and all, and he gives me the stuck in with such a
mortal motion that it is inevitable. And on the
275   answer, he pays you as surely as your feet hits the
ground they step on. They say he has been fencer to
the Sophy.

SIR ANDREW Pox on't, I'll not meddle with him.

SIR TOBY Ay, but he will not now be pacified. Fabian can
280   scarce hold him yonder.

---

245 competent sufficient   **247 that** i.e. the duel   **249 meddle** get involved   **250 forswear … you** cease to wear a sword   **252 office** task   **know of** inquire from   **259 mortal arbitrement** fight to the death   **262 Nothing … promise** not at all as extraordinary   **read** judge   **263 form** appearance   **like** likely   **270 mettle** spirit/courage   **272 firago** virago, female fighter   **pass** bout (of fencing)   **273 stuck in** fencing thrust   **274 mortal** fatal   **motion** fencing manoeuvre   **inevitable** unavoidable   **275 answer** return hit   **pays you** strikes you in return   **276 to** in the service of   **277 Sophy** Shah of Persia   **278 Pox** plague   **280 hold** restrain

SIR ANDREW Plague on't, an I thought he had been
valiant and so cunning in fence, I'd have seen him
damned ere I'd have challenged him. Let him let the
matter slip, and I'll give him my horse, grey Capilet.

285 SIR TOBY I'll make the motion. Stand here, make a good   *Aside*
show on't.— This shall end without the perdition of
souls. Marry, I'll ride your horse as well as I ride you.

Enter Fabian and Viola

I have his horse to take up the quarrel. I have   *Aside to Fabian*
persuaded him the youth's a devil.

290 FABIAN He is as horribly conceited of him, and pants and
looks pale, as if a bear were at his heels.

SIR TOBY There's no remedy, sir, he will fight with you   *To Viola*
for's oath sake. Marry, he hath better bethought him
of his quarrel, and he finds that now scarce to be

295 worth talking of: therefore draw for the supportance
of his vow. He protests he will not hurt you.

VIOLA Pray God defend me! A little thing would make me   *Aside*
tell them how much I lack of a man.

FABIAN Give ground if you see him furious.   *To Viola*

300 SIR TOBY Come, Sir Andrew, there's no remedy. The
gentleman will, for his honour's sake, have one bout
with you. He cannot by the duello avoid it. But he
has promised me, as he is a gentleman and a soldier,
he will not hurt you. Come on, to't.

305 SIR ANDREW Pray God he keep his oath!

Enter Antonio

VIOLA I do assure you, 'tis against my will.   *To Fabian/They draw*

ANTONIO Put up your sword. If this young gentleman   *their swords*
Have done offence, I take the fault on me.
If you offend him, I for him defy you.

310 SIR TOBY You, sir? Why, what are you?

ANTONIO One, sir, that for his love dares yet do more
Than you have heard him brag to you he will.

SIR TOBY Nay, if you be an undertaker, I am for you.   *They draw*

Enter Officers

FABIAN O, good Sir Toby, hold! Here come the officers.

315 SIR TOBY I'll be with you anon.   *To Antonio*

---

282 **cunning** skilful   **fence** fencing   283 **ere** before   285 **motion** offer   286 **perdition of souls** i.e. loss
of life   **perdition** destruction, damnation   287 **ride** i.e. make a fool of   288 **take up** settle   290 **horribly
conceited** has just as terrifying an idea   293 **for's oath** for his oath's   294 **quarrel** cause of complaint
295 **supportance** upholding   296 **protests** declares/vows   297 **A . . . would** it wouldn't take much to
(**thing** plays on the sense of 'penis')   302 **duello** established duelling code   307 **up** away   313 **undertaker**
one who takes on a task/challenger   **for** ready for   315 **anon** shortly

VIOLA Pray, sir, put your sword up, if you please.   *To Sir Andrew*
SIR ANDREW Marry, will I, sir. And for that I promised
  you, I'll be as good as my word. He will bear you
  easily and reins well.
320 **FIRST OFFICER** This is the man; do thy office.   *Indicates Antonio*
SECOND OFFICER Antonio, I arrest thee at the suit of
  Count Orsino.
ANTONIO You do mistake me, sir.
FIRST OFFICER No, sir, no jot. I know your favour well,
325   Though now you have no sea-cap on your head.
  Take him away: he knows I know him well.
ANTONIO I must obey.— This comes with seeking you.   *To Viola*
  But there's no remedy, I shall answer it.
  What will you do, now my necessity
330   Makes me to ask you for my purse? It grieves me
  Much more for what I cannot do for you
  Than what befalls myself. You stand amazed;
  But be of comfort.
SECOND OFFICER Come, sir, away.
335 **ANTONIO** I must entreat of you some of that money.   *To Viola*
VIOLA What money, sir?
  For the fair kindness you have showed me here,
  And part being prompted by your present trouble,
  Out of my lean and low ability
340   I'll lend you something. My having is not much.
  I'll make division of my present with you.
  Hold, there's half my coffer.   *Offers money*
ANTONIO Will you deny me now?
  Is't possible that my deserts to you
345   Can lack persuasion? Do not tempt my misery,
  Lest that it make me so unsound a man
  As to upbraid you with those kindnesses
  That I have done for you.
VIOLA I know of none,
350   Nor know I you by voice or any feature.
  I hate ingratitude more in a man
  Than lying, vainness, babbling, drunkenness,
  Or any taint of vice whose strong corruption
  Inhabits our frail blood.

---

317 **for that** as for what   318 **He** i.e. Capilet, the horse   319 **reins** is obedient, responds to the
reins   321 **suit** order/request   324 **favour** face   328 **answer** be accountable for   332 **amazed** shocked/
bewildered   338 **part** in part   340 **having** fortune   341 **present** available resources   342 **coffer**
money   343 **deny** reject/disown   344 **deserts** worthy deeds   345 **lack persuasion** fail to persuade you
to help me   **tempt** try   346 **unsound** morally weak/inadequate   352 **vainness** ostentation

355 **ANTONIO** O heavens themselves!

SECOND OFFICER Come, sir, I pray you go.

ANTONIO Let me speak a little. This youth that you see
here
I snatched one half out of the jaws of death,
Relieved him with such sanctity of love,
360 And to his image, which methought did promise
Most venerable worth, did I devotion.

FIRST OFFICER What's that to us? The time goes by.
Away!

ANTONIO But O, how vile an idol proves this god.
365 Thou hast, Sebastian, done good feature shame.
In nature there's no blemish but the mind.
None can be called deformed but the unkind.
Virtue is beauty, but the beauteous evil
Are empty trunks o'erflourished by the devil.

370 **FIRST OFFICER** The man grows mad. Away with him!
Come, come, sir.

ANTONIO Lead me on.   *Exit [with Officers]*

VIOLA Methinks his words do from such passion fly,   *Aside*
That he believes himself, so do not I.
375 Prove true, imagination, O, prove true,
That I, dear brother, be now ta'en for you!

SIR TOBY Come hither, knight. Come hither, Fabian.
We'll whisper o'er a couplet or two of most sage
saws.   *They stand aside*
380 **VIOLA** He named Sebastian. I my brother know
Yet living in my glass, even such and so
In favour was my brother, and he went
Still in this fashion, colour, ornament,
For him I imitate. O, if it prove,
385 Tempests are kind and salt waves fresh in love. *[Exit]*

SIR TOBY A very dishonest paltry boy, and more a
coward than a hare. His dishonesty appears in
leaving his friend here in necessity and denying
him. And for his cowardship, ask Fabian.
390 **FABIAN** A coward, a most devout coward, religious in it.

SIR ANDREW 'Slid, I'll after him again and beat him.

---

359 **sanctity** holiness   360 **image** appearance (plays on the sense of 'religious icon')   361 **venerable
worth** worthy to be venerated   365 **feature** physical appearance   367 **unkind** cruel/unnatural
369 **trunks** chests/bodies   **o'erflourished** richly decorated/made outwardly beautiful   378 **sage** solemn/
dignified   379 **saws** sayings   381 **glass** mirrored reflection/image   382 **favour** appearance   **went** went
about   383 **Still** always   **ornament** clothing, adornments   384 **prove** i.e. to be true   386 **dishonest**
dishonourable   **a coward** cowardly   390 **religious** devout   391 **'Slid** by God's eyelid (common oath)

SIR TOBY Do, cuff him soundly, but never draw thy
    sword.
SIR ANDREW An I do not—
395   FABIAN Come, let's see the event.
SIR TOBY I dare lay any money 'twill be nothing yet.

Exeunt

Act 4 Scene 1   *running scene 14*

Enter Sebastian and Clown [Feste]

FESTE Will you make me believe that I am not sent for
    you?
SEBASTIAN Go to, go to, thou art a foolish fellow.
    Let me be clear of thee.
5   FESTE Well held out, i'faith! No, I do not know you, nor I
    am not sent to you by my lady, to bid you come
    speak with her, nor your name is not Master Cesario,
    nor this is not my nose neither. Nothing that is so is
    so.
10   SEBASTIAN I prithee vent thy folly somewhere else. Thou
    know'st not me.
FESTE Vent my folly! He has heard that word of some
    great man and now applies it to a fool. Vent my folly!
    I am afraid this great lubber the world will prove a
15   cockney. I prithee now ungird thy strangeness and
    tell me what I shall vent to my lady. Shall I vent to
    her that thou art coming?
SEBASTIAN I prithee, foolish Greek, depart from me.   *Gives money*
    There's money for thee. If you tarry longer, I shall
20   give worse payment.
FESTE By my troth, thou hast an open hand. These wise
    men that give fools money get themselves a good
    report — after fourteen years' purchase.
Enter Andrew, Toby and Fabian
SIR ANDREW Now, sir, have I met you again? There's for *Strikes Sebastian*
25   you.
SEBASTIAN Why, there's for thee, and there, and there. *Beats Sir Andrew*
    Are all the people mad?

---

395 event outcome   **396 yet** after all   **4.1**   **5 held out** kept up   **10 vent** utter, let out   **12 of** from
14 lubber clumsy idiot   **15 cockney** pampered child/affected, effeminate fellow   **ungird** take off
strangeness aloofness   **18 Greek** buffoon/speaker of gibberish   **19 tarry** linger   **20 worse payment** i.e.
blows   **21 open** generous (with money or blows)   **23 report** reputation   **fourteen years' purchase** i.e. a
large investment of time and money

SIR TOBY Hold, sir, or I'll throw your dagger o'er the
house.

30 **FESTE** This will I tell my lady straight. I would not be in
some of your coats for twopence.   [*Exit*]

SIR TOBY Come on, sir, hold.

SIR ANDREW Nay, let him alone. I'll go another way to
work with him. I'll have an action of battery against
35 him, if there be any law in Illyria. Though I struck
him first, yet it's no matter for that.

SEBASTIAN Let go thy hand.

SIR TOBY Come, sir, I will not let you go. Come, my
young soldier, put up your iron. You are well fleshed.
40 Come on.

SEBASTIAN I will be free from thee. What wouldst thou
now? If thou darest tempt me further, draw thy
sword.

SIR TOBY What, what? Nay, then I must have an ounce
45 or two of this malapert blood from you.

Enter Olivia

OLIVIA Hold, Toby. On thy life I charge thee, hold!

SIR TOBY Madam!

OLIVIA Will it be ever thus? Ungracious wretch,
Fit for the mountains and the barbarous caves,
50 Where manners ne'er were preached! Out of my
       sight!—
Be not offended, dear Cesario.—
Rudesby, be gone!
                    [*Exeunt Sir Toby, Sir Andrew and Fabian*]
                         I prithee, gentle friend,
Let thy fair wisdom, not thy passion, sway
In this uncivil and unjust extent
55 Against thy peace. Go with me to my house,
And hear thou there how many fruitless pranks
This ruffian hath botched up, that thou thereby
Mayst smile at this. Thou shalt not choose but go.
Do not deny. Beshrew his soul for me,
60 He started one poor heart of mine in thee.

SEBASTIAN What relish is in this? How runs the stream?   *Aside*
Or I am mad, or else this is a dream.

---

30 straight at once   **in ... coats** in your position   **32 hold** restrain yourself   **34 action of battery** lawsuit
for assault   **39 iron** dagger/sword   **fleshed** initiated into fighting   **45 malapert** impudent   **52 Rudesby**
ruffian   **friend** friend/lover   **54 uncivil** barbarous   **extent** assault   **57 botched up** patched together
59 Beshrew curse   **60 started** startled/drove from cover   **heart** puns on 'hart'   **61 relish** meaning
(literally, 'taste')   **62 Or** either

Let fancy still my sense in Lethe steep.
If it be thus to dream, still let me sleep!
65   OLIVIA Nay, come, I prithee. Would thou'dst be ruled by
me!
SEBASTIAN Madam, I will.
OLIVIA O, say so, and so be!   *Exeunt*

Act 4 Scene 2   *running scene 15*

Enter Maria and Clown [Feste]

MARIA Nay, I prithee put on this gown and this beard.   *Hands him a*
Make him believe thou art Sir Topas the curate. Do it *gown and beard*
quickly. I'll call Sir Toby the whilst.   [*Exit*]
FESTE Well, I'll put it on, and I will dissemble myself in't,
5   and I would I were the first that ever dissembled in
such a gown. I am not tall enough to become the   *Puts on gown*
function well, nor lean enough to be thought a good   *and beard*
student. But to be said an honest man and a good
housekeeper goes as fairly as to say a careful man
10   and a great scholar. The competitors enter.
Enter Toby [and Maria]
SIR TOBY Jove bless thee, Master Parson.
FESTE *Bonos dies,* Sir Toby. For, as the old hermit of
Prague that never saw pen and ink very wittily said
to a niece of King Gorboduc, 'That that is, is.' So I,
15   being Master Parson, am Master Parson; for what is
'that' but 'that', and 'is' but 'is'?
SIR TOBY To him, Sir Topas.
FESTE What, ho, I say? Peace in this prison.
SIR TOBY The knave counterfeits well, a good knave.
20   MALVOLIO Who calls there?   *Within*
FESTE Sir Topas the curate, who comes to visit Malvolio
the lunatic.
MALVOLIO Sir Topas, Sir Topas, good Sir Topas, go to my
lady.

---

63 **fancy** imagination   **Lethe** river of forgetfulness in the classical underworld   64 **still** always   65 **Would thou'dst** if only you would   **4.2   2 Sir** respectful title for priest   **Topas** topaz, a precious stone, was supposed to cure madness; also proverbial for a puritan priest   **curate** parish priest   **3 the whilst** in the meantime   **4 dissemble** disguise   **5 dissembled** feigned, deceived   **6 become** suit   **7 function** task/role (of priest)   **8 said** reputed   **9 housekeeper** host   **goes as fairly** sounds as good   **careful** painstaking/conscientious   **10 competitors** conspirators, partners in crime   **12 *Bonos dies*** 'good day' (mock Latin/Spanish)   **old...Prague** an invented authority   **13 never...ink** was illiterate   **14 King Gorboduc** legendary British king

25   FESTE Out, hyperbolical fiend! How vexest thou this
       man! Talkest thou nothing but of ladies?
     SIR TOBY Well said, Master Parson.
     MALVOLIO Sir Topas, never was man thus wronged.
       Good Sir Topas, do not think I am mad. They have
30   laid me here in hideous darkness.
     FESTE Fie, thou dishonest Satan! I call thee by the most
       modest terms, for I am one of those gentle ones that
       will use the devil himself with courtesy. Sayest thou
       that house is dark?
35   MALVOLIO As hell, Sir Topas.
     FESTE Why it hath bay windows transparent as
       barricadoes, and the clerestories toward the south
       north are as lustrous as ebony, and yet complainest
       thou of obstruction?
40   MALVOLIO I am not mad, Sir Topas. I say to you, this
       house is dark.
     FESTE Madman, thou errest. I say there is no darkness
       but ignorance, in which thou art more puzzled than
       the Egyptians in their fog.
45   MALVOLIO I say, this house is as dark as ignorance,
       though ignorance were as dark as hell; and I say
       there was never man thus abused. I am no more mad
       than you are. Make the trial of it in any constant
       question.
50   FESTE What is the opinion of Pythagoras concerning
       wild fowl?
     MALVOLIO That the soul of our grandam might happily
       inhabit a bird.
     FESTE What think'st thou of his opinion?
55   MALVOLIO I think nobly of the soul, and no way approve
       his opinion.
     FESTE Fare thee well. Remain thou still in darkness.
       Thou shalt hold th'opinion of Pythagoras ere I will
       allow of thy wits, and fear to kill a woodcock, lest
60   thou dispossess the soul of thy grandam. Fare thee
       well.

---

25 hyperbolical immoderate/vehement/raging   **fiend** evil spirit (supposedly possessing Malvolio)   **vexest** torment   **32 modest terms** mild expressions   **34 house** i.e. room   **37 barricadoes** barricades   **clerestories** upper windows   **43 puzzled** bewildered   **44 Egyptians . . . fog** in the Bible, God punished the Egyptians with three days of darkness   **47 abused** wronged/maltreated   **48 constant** decided/consistent/logical   **49 question** discussion, debate   **50 Pythagoras** ancient Greek philosopher who believed in the transmigration of souls from humans to animals   **52 grandam** grandmother   **happily** perhaps (though may play on adverbial sense)   **59 allow . . . wits** acknowledge you are sane   **woodcock** proverbially stupid and easily caught bird

MALVOLIO Sir Topas, Sir Topas!

SIR TOBY My most exquisite Sir Topas!

FESTE Nay, I am for all waters.

65 MARIA Thou mightst have done this without thy beard
and gown. He sees thee not.

SIR TOBY To him in thine own voice, and bring me word
how thou findest him. I would we were well rid of
this knavery. If he may be conveniently delivered,

70 I would he were, for I am now so far in offence with
my niece that I cannot pursue with any safety this
sport to the upshot. Come by and by to my chamber.

Exeunt [Sir Toby and Maria]

FESTE 'Hey, Robin, jolly Robin,   *Sings*
Tell me how thy lady does.'

75 MALVOLIO Fool!

FESTE 'My lady is unkind, perdy.'   *Sings*

MALVOLIO Fool!

FESTE 'Alas, why is she so?'   *Sings*

MALVOLIO Fool, I say!

80 FESTE 'She loves another'— Who calls, ha?   *Sings*

MALVOLIO Good fool, as ever thou wilt deserve well at
my hand, help me to a candle, and pen, ink and
paper. As I am a gentleman, I will live to be thankful
to thee for't.

85 FESTE Master Malvolio?

MALVOLIO Ay, good fool.

FESTE Alas, sir, how fell you besides your five wits?

MALVOLIO Fool, there was never man so notoriously
abused. I am as well in my wits, fool, as thou art.

90 FESTE But as well? Then you are mad indeed, if you be
no better in your wits than a fool.

MALVOLIO They have here propertied me, keep me in
darkness, send ministers to me, asses, and do all they
can to face me out of my wits.

95 FESTE Advise you what you say. The minister is here.—
Malvolio, Malvolio, thy wits the heavens restore!   *As Sir Topas*
Endeavour thyself to sleep, and leave thy vain
bibble babble.

---

63 **exquisite** ingenious/exact (in imitation)   64 **am ... waters** can turn my hand to anything   67 **To** go to   69 **delivered** liberated   72 **upshot** final stroke, conclusion   **by and by** straight away   76 **perdy** by God (from French *par dieu*)   87 **besides** out of   **five wits** mental faculties: common sense, fantasy, judgement, memory and imagination   88 **notoriously** evidently/outrageously   90 **But** only   92 **propertied** packed away like a piece of furniture/a stage prop   94 **face** bully   95 **Advise you** be careful/consider   98 **bibble babble** idle chatter

MALVOLIO Sir Topas!

100 **FESTE** Maintain no words with him, good fellow.—   *As Sir Topas*
Who, I, sir? Not I, sir. God buy you, good Sir   *As himself*
Topas.—
Marry, amen.—   *As Sir Topas*
I will, sir, I will.   *As himself*

105 **MALVOLIO** Fool, fool, fool, I say!

FESTE Alas, sir, be patient. What say you, sir? I am shent
for speaking to you.

MALVOLIO Good fool, help me to some light and some
paper. I tell thee I am as well in my wits as any man

110 in Illyria.

FESTE Well-a-day that you were, sir.

MALVOLIO By this hand, I am. Good fool, some ink, paper
and light, and convey what I will set down to my
lady. It shall advantage thee more than ever the

115 bearing of letter did.

FESTE I will help you to't. But tell me true, are you not
mad indeed? Or do you but counterfeit?

MALVOLIO Believe me, I am not. I tell thee true.

FESTE Nay, I'll ne'er believe a madman till I see his

120 brains. I will fetch you light and paper and ink.

MALVOLIO Fool, I'll requite it in the highest degree. I
prithee be gone.

FESTE   I am gone, sir,
And anon, sir,   *Sings*

125 I'll be with you again,
In a trice,
Like to the old Vice,
Your need to sustain,
Who, with dagger of lath,

130 In his rage and his wrath,
Cries 'Aha!' to the devil,
Like a mad lad,
Pare thy nails, dad.
Adieu, goodman devil.   *Exit*

---

101 **God buy you** goodbye, literally 'God be with you'   106 **shent** rebuked   111 **Well-a-day** alas/
would   121 **requite** repay   126 **a trice** an instant   127 **Vice** buffoon/comic character in old morality
plays   129 **dagger of lath** the weapon of the Vice character   **lath** thin wood   133 **Pare thy nails**
probably a comic routine in morality plays   **Pare** trim   **dad** the Vice was sometimes portrayed as the devil's
son   134 **goodman** title for someone below the rank of gentleman

Act 4 Scene 3

Enter Sebastian

SEBASTIAN This is the air, that is the glorious sun,
    This pearl she gave me, I do feel't and see't.   *Holds up a pearl*
    And though 'tis wonder that enwraps me thus,
    Yet 'tis not madness. Where's Antonio, then?
5   I could not find him at the Elephant.
    Yet there he was, and there I found this credit,
    That he did range the town to seek me out.
    His counsel now might do me golden service,
    For though my soul disputes well with my sense
10   That this may be some error but no madness,
    Yet doth this accident and flood of fortune
    So far exceed all instance, all discourse,
    That I am ready to distrust mine eyes
    And wrangle with my reason that persuades me
15   To any other trust but that I am mad,
    Or else the lady's mad; yet, if 'twere so,
    She could not sway her house, command her
      followers,
    Take and give back affairs and their dispatch
    With such a smooth, discreet and stable bearing
20   As I perceive she does. There's something in't
    That is deceivable. But here the lady comes.

Enter Olivia and Priest

OLIVIA Blame not this haste of mine. If you mean well,
    Now go with me and with this holy man
    Into the chantry by: there, before him,
25   And underneath that consecrated roof,
    Plight me the full assurance of your faith,
    That my most jealous and too doubtful soul
    May live at peace. He shall conceal it
    Whiles you are willing it shall come to note,
30   What time we will our celebration keep
    According to my birth. What do you say?

SEBASTIAN I'll follow this good man, and go with you,
    And having sworn truth, ever will be true.

4.3   6 was had been   **credit** report   **7 range** roam   **9 disputes well** i.e. agrees   **11 accident** unforeseen event   **12 instance** precedent   **discourse** rationality   **14 wrangle** argue   **15 trust** belief   **17 sway her house** govern her household   **18 Take … dispatch** deal with matters of household business   **21 deceivable** deceptive   **24 chantry** private chapel   **by** nearby   **26 Plight … faith** pledge your love (in a binding betrothal)   **27 jealous** anxious, uncertain, wary   **29 Whiles** until   **note** public knowledge   **30 What** at which   **celebration** i.e. marriage   **31 birth** social status

OLIVIA Then lead the way, good father, and heavens so
    shine,
35   That they may fairly note this act of mine!   *Exeunt*

Act 5 Scene 1

Enter Clown [Feste] and Fabian

FABIAN Now, as thou lovest me, let me see his letter.
FESTE Good Master Fabian, grant me another request.
FABIAN Anything.
FESTE Do not desire to see this letter.
5   **FABIAN** This is to give a dog and in recompense desire my
    dog again.
Enter Duke [Orsino], Viola, Curio and Lords
ORSINO Belong you to the lady Olivia, friends?
FESTE Ay, sir, we are some of her trappings.
ORSINO I know thee well. How dost thou, my good
10   fellow?
FESTE Truly, sir, the better for my foes and the worse for
    my friends.
ORSINO Just the contrary, the better for thy friends.
FESTE No, sir, the worse.
15   **ORSINO** How can that be?
FESTE Marry, sir, they praise me and make an ass of me.
    Now my foes tell me plainly I am an ass: so that by
    my foes, sir, I profit in the knowledge of myself, and
    by my friends I am abused: so that, conclusions to be
20   as kisses, if your four negatives make your two
    affirmatives, why then, the worse for my friends and
    the better for my foes.
ORSINO Why, this is excellent.
FESTE By my troth, sir, no, though it please you to be
25   one of my friends.
ORSINO Thou shalt not be the worse for me. There's   *Gives a coin*
    gold.
FESTE But that it would be double-dealing, sir, I would
    you could make it another.
30   **ORSINO** O, you give me ill counsel.

35 **fairly note** observe with favour   **5.1   5 This . . . again** seemingly refers to the anecdote about Elizabeth I
and her kinsman Dr Boleyn; she asked for his dog and promised him anything in return, upon which he
asked for the animal back   **8 trappings** ornaments/bits and pieces   **11 for** because of   **19 abused**
deceived   **so . . . affirmatives** if the outcome is like the response to a request for a kiss, where 'no, no, no, no'
means 'yes, yes'   **24 though** even though   **25 friends** i.e. one who gives him **praise**   **28 But** except for the
fact   **double-dealing** duplicity/giving twice

FESTE Put your grace in your pocket, sir, for this once,
and let your flesh and blood obey it.

ORSINO Well, I will be so much a sinner to be a double-   *Gives another*
dealer. There's another.   *coin*

35 FESTE *Primo, secundo, tertio*, is a good play, and the old
saying is, the third pays for all. The triplex, sir, is a
good tripping measure, or the bells of Saint Bennet,
sir, may put you in mind: one, two, three.

ORSINO You can fool no more money out of me at this
40 throw. If you will let your lady know I am here to
speak with her, and bring her along with you, it may
awake my bounty further.

FESTE Marry, sir, lullaby to your bounty till I come
again. I go, sir. But I would not have you to think
45 that my desire of having is the sin of covetousness.
But as you say, sir, let your bounty take a nap, I will
awake it anon.   *Exit*

Enter Antonio and Officers

VIOLA Here comes the man, sir, that did rescue me.

ORSINO That face of his I do remember well,
50 Yet, when I saw it last, it was besmeared
As black as Vulcan in the smoke of war.
A bawbling vessel was he captain of,
For shallow draught and bulk unprizeable,
With which such scathful grapple did he make
55 With the most noble bottom of our fleet,
That very envy and the tongue of loss
Cried fame and honour on him. What's the matter?

FIRST OFFICER Orsino, this is that Antonio
That took the *Phoenix* and her fraught from Candy,
60 And this is he that did the *Tiger* board
When your young nephew Titus lost his leg;
Here in the streets, desperate of shame and state,
In private brabble did we apprehend him.

---

31 your grace favour/virtue (plays on the customary way of addressing a duke)   in your pocket i.e. to hide it/to give money   32 flesh and blood human instincts/frailty   it i.e. the ill counsel   33 to as to
35 *Primo, secundo, tertio* 'first, second, third' (Latin)   play game   36 third…all i.e. third time lucky (proverbial)   triplex triple time in music   37 tripping nimble, skipping   measure stately dance/music
Saint Bennet church of Saint Benedict   40 throw roll of the dice/occasion   43 lullaby i.e. farewell
51 Vulcan Roman god of fire, and the gods' blacksmith   52 bawbling trifling   53 For (trifling) because of   draught depth of water required to float the ship   unprizeable of little value   54 scathful damaging   grapple close fighting, attempts to board another ship   55 bottom ship (literally, ship's hull)   56 very even   envy malice, i.e. his enemies   loss defeat   59 *Phoenix* name of Illyrian ship   fraught cargo
Candy Candia, modern Heraklion, a port in Crete   60 *Tiger* name of Illyrian ship   62 desperate disregarding   63 brabble brawl

VIOLA He did me kindness, sir, drew on my side,
65   But in conclusion put strange speech upon me.
         I know not what 'twas but distraction.
ORSINO Notable pirate! Thou salt-water thief!
         What foolish boldness brought thee to their mercies,
         Whom thou, in terms so bloody and so dear,
70   Hast made thine enemies?
ANTONIO Orsino, noble sir,
         Be pleased that I shake off these names you give me.
         Antonio never yet was thief or pirate,
         Though I confess, on base and ground enough,
75   Orsino's enemy. A witchcraft drew me hither.
         That most ingrateful boy there by your side
         From the rude sea's enragèd and foamy mouth
         Did I redeem. A wreck past hope he was.
         His life I gave him and did thereto add
80   My love, without retention or restraint,
         All his in dedication. For his sake
         Did I expose myself — pure for his love —
         Into the danger of this adverse town,
         Drew to defend him when he was beset,
85   Where being apprehended, his false cunning —
         Not meaning to partake with me in danger —
         Taught him to face me out of his acquaintance,
         And grew a twenty years removèd thing
         While one would wink, denied me mine own purse,
90   Which I had recommended to his use
         Not half an hour before.
VIOLA How can this be?
ORSINO When came he to this town?
ANTONIO Today, my lord. And for three months before,
95   No interim, not a minute's vacancy,
         Both day and night did we keep company.
Enter Olivia and Attendants
ORSINO Here comes the countess. Now heaven walks on
         earth.
         But for thee, fellow — fellow, thy words are madness.

---

64 on my side (his sword) in my defence   **65 put ... me** spoke to me strangely   **66 but distraction** if not
madness   **67 Notable** notorious   **69 bloody** bloodthirsty   **dear** grievous, severe   **72 Be ... I** allow me
to   **74 base** basis   **77 rude** rough   **80 retention** reservation   **81 All ... dedication** dedicated wholly to
him   **82 pure** purely   **83 adverse** hostile   **87 face ... acquaintance** deny he knew me   **88 grew ...**
wink in the space of a moment he behaved as if we had not seen each other for twenty years
90 recommended committed   **98 But for** as for

Three months this youth hath tended upon me.
100 But more of that anon. Take him aside.
OLIVIA What would my lord, but that he may not have,
Wherein Olivia may seem serviceable?
Cesario, you do not keep promise with me.
VIOLA Madam?
105 ORSINO Gracious Olivia—
OLIVIA What do you say, Cesario? Good my lord—
VIOLA My lord would speak, my duty hushes me.
OLIVIA If it be aught to the old tune, my lord,
It is as fat and fulsome to mine ear
110 As howling after music.
ORSINO Still so cruel?
OLIVIA Still so constant, lord.
ORSINO What, to perverseness? You uncivil lady,
To whose ingrate and unauspicious altars
115 My soul the faithfull'st offerings hath breathed out
That e'er devotion tendered! What shall I do?
OLIVIA Even what it please my lord that shall become
him.
ORSINO Why should I not, had I the heart to do it,
Like to th'Egyptian thief at point of death,
120 Kill what I love? — a savage jealousy
That sometimes savours nobly. But hear me this:
Since you to non-regardance cast my faith,
And that I partly know the instrument
That screws me from my true place in your favour,
125 Live you the marble-breasted tyrant still.
But this your minion, whom I know you love,
And whom, by heaven I swear, I tender dearly,
Him will I tear out of that cruel eye,
Where he sits crownèd in his master's spite.
130 Come, boy, with me. My thoughts are ripe in
mischief:
I'll sacrifice the lamb that I do love,
To spite a raven's heart within a dove.   *Starts to leave*

---

101 but...have except that which I refuse him, i.e. love   106 lord if addressed to Viola, 'husband' (Viola uses the sense of 'master')   108 aught anything   109 fat gross   fulsome distasteful, nauseating 113 uncivil uncivilized   114 ingrate ungrateful   unauspicious ill-omened, unpromising   116 tendered offered (may play on 'tender', i.e. loving, gentle)   117 Even what whatever/exactly what   become suit   119 Egyptian thief character from a Greek romance who tried to kill a captive he loved when his own life was threatened   121 savours nobly has a taste of nobility   122 non-regardance disrespect/lack of attention   123 that since   124 screws forces   126 minion favourite/darling   127 tender care for/ value   129 in...spite to the vexation of his master   130 ripe in mischief ready to do harm

VIOLA And I, most jocund, apt and willingly,
    To do you rest, a thousand deaths would die.   *Starts to leave*
135 OLIVIA Where goes Cesario?
VIOLA After him I love
    More than I love these eyes, more than my life,
    More, by all mores, than e'er I shall love wife.
    If I do feign, you witnesses above
140   Punish my life for tainting of my love!
OLIVIA Ay me, detested! How am I beguiled!
VIOLA Who does beguile you? Who does do you wrong?
OLIVIA Hast thou forgot thyself? Is it so long?
    Call forth the holy father.   [*Exit an Attendant*]
145 ORSINO Come, away!   *To Viola*
OLIVIA Whither, my lord? Cesario, husband, stay.
ORSINO Husband?
OLIVIA Ay, husband. Can he that deny?
ORSINO Her husband, sirrah?
150 VIOLA No, my lord, not I.
OLIVIA Alas, it is the baseness of thy fear
    That makes thee strangle thy propriety
    Fear not, Cesario, take thy fortunes up.
    Be that thou know'st thou art, and then thou art
165   As great as that thou fear'st.
Enter Priest
    O, welcome, father!
    Father, I charge thee by thy reverence
    Here to unfold, though lately we intended
    To keep in darkness what occasion now
160   Reveals before 'tis ripe, what thou dost know
    Hath newly passed between this youth and me.
PRIEST A contract of eternal bond of love,
    Confirmed by mutual joinder of your hands,
    Attested by the holy close of lips,
165   Strengthened by interchangement of your rings,
    And all the ceremony of this compact
    Sealed in my function, by my testimony.
    Since when, my watch hath told me, toward my
        grave
    I have travelled but two hours.

---

133 jocund cheerful apt readily   134 To...rest in order to give you ease   138 mores such
comparisons 140 tainting of discrediting   141 beguiled deceived   149 sirrah sir (contemptuous; used to
an inferior)   151 baseness cowardice/lowly nature   152 strangle stifle propriety real identity
154 that that which   155 that thou fear'st him you fear, i.e. Orsino   158 unfold reveal   163 joinder
joining   164 close meeting   166 compact agreement   167 Sealed...function certified by my priestly
authority   168 watch clock

170   ORSINO O thou dissembling cub! What wilt thou be   *To Viola*
        When time hath sowed a grizzle on thy case?
        Or will not else thy craft so quickly grow
        That thine own trip shall be thine overthrow?
        Farewell, and take her; but direct thy feet
175   Where thou and I henceforth may never meet.
      VIOLA My lord, I do protest—
      OLIVIA O, do not swear!
        Hold little faith, though thou hast too much fear.
      Enter Sir Andrew   *His head bleeding*
      SIR ANDREW For the love of God, a surgeon! Send one
180   presently to Sir Toby.
      OLIVIA What's the matter?
      SIR ANDREW H'as broke my head across and has given
        Sir Toby a bloody coxcomb too. For the love of God,
        your help! I had rather than forty pound I were at
185   home.
      OLIVIA Who has done this, Sir Andrew?
      SIR ANDREW The count's gentleman, one Cesario. We
        took him for a coward, but he's the very devil
        incardinate.
190   ORSINO My gentleman, Cesario?
      SIR ANDREW 'Od's lifelings, here he is! You broke my
        head for nothing, and that that I did, I was set on to
        do't by Sir Toby.
      VIOLA Why do you speak to me? I never hurt you.
195   You drew your sword upon me without cause,
        But I bespake you fair, and hurt you not.
      Enter Toby and Clown [Feste]   *Sir Toby wounded*
      SIR ANDREW If a bloody coxcomb be a hurt, you have
        hurt me. I think you set nothing by a bloody
        coxcomb. Here comes Sir Toby halting. You shall
200   hear more. But if he had not been in drink, he would
        have tickled you othergates than he did.
      ORSINO How now, gentleman? How is't with you?
      SIR TOBY That's all one: h'as hurt me, and there's th'end
        on't. Sot, didst see Dick surgeon, sot?

---

171 grizzle sprinkling of grey hair   **case** (animal) skin   **172 craft** cunning   **173 trip** wrestling move to
throw opponent   **176 protest** declare/swear   **178 Hold little faith** keep some part of your promise
180 presently immediately   **182 H'as broke** he has cut   **183 coxcomb** head (with suggestion of fool's
cap resembling a cock's crest)   **189 incardinate** incarnate   **191 'Od's lifelings** by God's little lives (mild
oath)   **198 set nothing by** think nothing of   **199 halting** limping   **200 in drink** drunk   **201 tickled** i.e.
beaten   **othergates** in another way, i.e. differently   **203 all one** doesn't matter   **there's th'end on't**
that's all there is to it   **204 sot** idiot/drunkard

205 FESTE O, he's drunk, Sir Toby, an hour agone. His eyes
were set at eight i'th'morning.

SIR TOBY Then he's a rogue, and a passy measures
pavin. I hate a drunken rogue.

OLIVIA Away with him! Who hath made this havoc with
210 them?

SIR ANDREW I'll help you, Sir Toby, because we'll be
dressed together.

SIR TOBY Will you help? An ass-head and a coxcomb
and a knave, a thin-faced knave, a gull!

215 OLIVIA Get him to bed, and let his hurt be looked to.
            [*Exeunt Feste, Fabian, Sir Toby and Sir Andrew*]
Enter Sebastian

SEBASTIAN I am sorry, madam, I have hurt your
            kinsman.
    But, had it been the brother of my blood,
    I must have done no less with wit and safety.
    You throw a strange regard upon me, and by that
220 I do perceive it hath offended you.
    Pardon me, sweet one, even for the vows
    We made each other but so late ago.

ORSINO One face, one voice, one habit, and two persons,
    A natural perspective, that is and is not!

225 SEBASTIAN Antonio, O my dear Antonio!
    How have the hours racked and tortured me,
    Since I have lost thee!

ANTONIO Sebastian are you?

SEBASTIAN Fear'st thou that, Antonio?

230 ANTONIO How have you made division of yourself?
    An apple cleft in two is not more twin
    Than these two creatures. Which is Sebastian?

OLIVIA Most wonderful!

SEBASTIAN Do I stand there? I never had a brother,   *Sees Viola*
235 Nor can there be that deity in my nature
    Of here and everywhere. I had a sister,
    Whom the blind waves and surges have devoured.
    Of charity, what kin are you to me?
    What countryman? What name? What parentage?

---

205 agone ago, past   **206 set** glazed/fixed/closed (**eight i'th'morning** may suggest the manner in which
the surgeon's eyes were fixed, rolling back, like the sun high in the morning sky)   **207 passy measures
pavin** stately dance, i.e. slow   **211 be dressed** bandaged   **213 coxcomb** fool   **214 gull** dupe/fool
217 brother . . . blood my own brother   **218 with . . . safety** in reasonable self-protection   **219 strange
regard** odd/distant look   **223 habit** clothing   **224 natural perspective** optical illusion produced by
nature   **226 racked** tormented   **229 Fear'st** doubt   **235 deity** godlike quality   **236 here and
everywhere** omnipresence   **237 blind** heedless   **238 Of charity** (tell me) out of kindness

240 VIOLA Of Messaline. Sebastian was my father,
         Such a Sebastian was my brother too,
         So went he suited to his watery tomb.
         If spirits can assume both form and suit
         You come to fright us.
245 SEBASTIAN A spirit I am indeed,
         But am in that dimension grossly clad
         Which from the womb I did participate.
         Were you a woman, as the rest goes even,
         I should my tears let fall upon your cheek,
250   And say 'Thrice-welcome, drownèd Viola!'
     VIOLA My father had a mole upon his brow.
     SEBASTIAN And so had mine.
     VIOLA And died that day when Viola from her birth
         Had numbered thirteen years.
255 SEBASTIAN O, that record is lively in my soul!
         He finished indeed his mortal act
         That day that made my sister thirteen years.
     VIOLA If nothing lets to make us happy both
         But this my masculine usurped attire,
260   Do not embrace me till each circumstance
         Of place, time, fortune, do cohere and jump
         That I am Viola — which to confirm,
         I'll bring you to a captain in this town,
         Where lie my maiden weeds, by whose gentle help
265   I was preserved to serve this noble count.
         All the occurrence of my fortune since
         Hath been between this lady and this lord.
     SEBASTIAN So comes it, lady, you have been mistook.   *To Olivia*
         But nature to her bias drew in that.
270   You would have been contracted to a maid,
         Nor are you therein, by my life, deceived,
         You are betrothed both to a maid and man.
     ORSINO Be not amazed; right noble is his blood.—   *To Olivia*
         If this be so, as yet the glass seems true,   *Aside?*
275   I shall have share in this most happy wreck.—
         Boy, thou hast said to me a thousand times   *To Viola*
         Thou never shouldst love woman like to me.

---

242 **suited** dressed   243 **form and suit** physical appearance and dress   246 **am ... clad** my body is
clothed with the flesh   247 **participate** have in common with all humanity   248 **the ... even** everything
else is in agreement   255 **record** memory   **lively** vivid, alive   258 **lets** hinders   261 **jump** coincide
264 **weeds** clothes   268 **mistook** mistaken   269 **to ... drew** inclined in the right direction (bowling
metaphor)   270 **contracted** betrothed   274 **glass** mirror/lens of optical instrument (**perspective**)
275 **happy** fortunate   277 **like to** as much as

VIOLA And all those sayings will I overswear;
And all those swearings keep as true in soul
280   As doth that orbèd continent the fire
That severs day from night.
ORSINO Give me thy hand,
And let me see thee in thy woman's weeds.
VIOLA The captain that did bring me first on shore
285   Hath my maid's garments. He upon some action
Is now in durance, at Malvolio's suit,
A gentleman, and follower of my lady's.
OLIVIA He shall enlarge him. Fetch Malvolio hither.
And yet, alas, now I remember me,
290   They say, poor gentleman, he's much distract.
Enter Clown [Feste] with a letter, and Fabian
A most extracting frenzy of mine own
From my remembrance clearly banished his.
How does he, sirrah?
FESTE Truly, madam, he holds Beelzebub at the stave's
295   end as well as a man in his case may do. H'as here
writ a letter to you; I should have given't you today
morning, but as a madman's epistles are no gospels,
so it skills not much when they are delivered.
OLIVIA Open't, and read it.
300 FESTE Look then to be well edified when the fool delivers
the madman. 'By the lord, madam'—   *Reads*
OLIVIA How now, art thou mad?
FESTE No, madam, I do but read madness. An your
ladyship will have it as it ought to be, you must allow
305   *vox*.
OLIVIA Prithee read i'thy right wits.
FESTE So I do, madonna. But to read his right wits is to
read thus: therefore perpend, my princess, and give
ear.
310 OLIVIA Read it you, sirrah.   *To Fabian, who takes the letter*
FABIAN *Reads*
'By the lord, madam, you wrong me, and the world
shall know it. Though you have put me into darkness

---

278 overswear swear again and again   **280 orbèd continent** spherical container, i.e. as the sun
keeps   **285 action** legal charge   **286 in durance** imprisoned   **288 enlarge** release   **289 remember me**
remember   **290 distract** mad   **291 extracting** distracting   **frenzy** agitation/madness   **292 From . . . his**
drove him from my memory   **294 Beelzebub** the devil   **the stave's end** at a distance   **296 today** i.e.
this   **297 epistles** letters/New Testament letters from the apostles   **gospels** truths/New Testament
records of Christ's life and teaching   **298 skills** matters   **delivered** handed over   **300 delivers** speaks the
words of   **305 vox** 'voice' (Latin), i.e. the correct manner of delivery (Feste has obviously read the words in a
'mad' style)   **307 read** discern   **right wits** true state of mind   **308 perpend** consider

and given your drunken cousin rule over me, yet
have I the benefit of my senses as well as your
315 ladyship. I have your own letter that induced me to
the semblance I put on; with the which I doubt not
but to do myself much right, or you much shame.
Think of me as you please. I leave my duty a little
unthought of and speak out of my injury.
320   The madly-used Malvolio.'

OLIVIA Did he write this?

FESTE Ay, madam.

ORSINO This savours not much of distraction.

OLIVIA See him delivered, Fabian, bring him hither.

                                              [*Exit Fabian*]
325 My lord, so please you, these things further thought
        on,
To think me as well a sister as a wife,
One day shall crown th'alliance on't, so please you,
Here at my house and at my proper cost.

ORSINO Madam, I am most apt t'embrace your offer.—
330 Your master quits you. And for your service done
        him,   *To Viola*
So much against the mettle of your sex,
So far beneath your soft and tender breeding,
And since you called me master for so long,
Here is my hand. You shall from this time be
335 Your master's mistress.

OLIVIA A sister! You are she.

Enter Malvolio [and Fabian]

ORSINO Is this the madman?

OLIVIA Ay, my lord, this same.—
How now, Malvolio?

340 **MALVOLIO** Madam, you have done me wrong,
Notorious wrong.

OLIVIA Have I, Malvolio? No.

MALVOLIO Lady, you have. Pray you peruse that letter.   *Hands her the*
You must not now deny it is your hand.   *letter*
345 Write from it, if you can, in hand or phrase,
Or say 'tis not your seal, not your invention.

---

316 semblance outward show   **the which** i.e. the letter   **318 duty** i.e. respectful behaviour of a
steward   **319 out…injury** as a wronged party   **324 delivered** released   **325 so** may it   **thought on**
considered   **326 as…wife** as good a sister-in-law as you'd hoped to regard me as a wife   **327 th'alliance**
the union (in a double wedding)   **328 proper** personal   **329 apt** ready   **330 quits** releases (from
service)   **331 mettle** natural disposition   **344 hand** handwriting   **345 from it** differently   **346 invention**
composition

You can say none of this. Well, grant it then,
And tell me, in the modesty of honour,
Why you have given me such clear lights of favour,
350 Bade me come smiling and cross-gartered to you,
To put on yellow stockings and to frown
Upon Sir Toby and the lighter people?
And, acting this in an obedient hope,
Why have you suffered me to be imprisoned,
355 Kept in a dark house, visited by the priest,
And made the most notorious geck and gull
That e'er invention played on? Tell me why.
OLIVIA Alas, Malvolio, this is not my writing,
Though, I confess, much like the character,
360 But out of question 'tis Maria's hand.
And now I do bethink me, it was she
First told me thou wast mad; then cam'st in smiling,
And in such forms which here were presupposed
Upon thee in the letter. Prithee be content.
365 This practice hath most shrewdly passed upon thee,
But when we know the grounds and authors of it,
Thou shalt be both the plaintiff and the judge
Of thine own cause.
FABIAN Good madam, hear me speak,
370 And let no quarrel nor no brawl to come
Taint the condition of this present hour,
Which I have wondered at. In hope it shall not,
Most freely I confess, myself and Toby
Set this device against Malvolio here,
375 Upon some stubborn and uncourteous parts
We had conceived against him. Maria writ
The letter at Sir Toby's great importance,
In recompense whereof he hath married her.
How with a sportful malice it was followed,
380 May rather pluck on laughter than revenge,
If that the injuries be justly weighed
That have on both sides passed.

---

348 modesty of honour name of all that is decent and honourable/restraint befitting your status
349 lights signals   **352 lighter** more frivolous/lesser   **353 acting** undertaking   **354 suffered** allowed
356 geck dupe/fool   **357 invention played on** trickery sported with   **359 character** style of writing
360 out of beyond   **362 cam'st** you came   **363 presupposed Upon** previously suggested to
365 practice plot/trick   **shrewdly** mischievously   **passed** been perpetrated   **371 condition** (happy)
circumstances   **372 wondered** marvelled   **375 Upon** because of   **uncourteous** unfriendly/uncivil
parts qualities/actions   **376 conceived against** imagined/discerned in   **377 importance** urging
379 sportful playful   **followed** followed up/carried out   **380 pluck on** induce   **381 If that** If

OLIVIA Alas, poor fool, how have they baffled thee!

FESTE Why, 'Some are born great, some achieve
385   greatness, and some have greatness thrown upon
         them.' I was one, sir, in this interlude; one Sir Topas,
         sir, but that's all one. 'By the Lord, fool, I am not mad.'
         But do you remember? Madam, why laugh you at
         such a barren rascal? An you smile not, he's gagged.'
390   And thus the whirligig of time brings in his revenges.

MALVOLIO I'll be revenged on the whole pack of you.
                                                      [*Exit*]

OLIVIA He hath been most notoriously abused.

ORSINO Pursue him and entreat him to a peace.
         He hath not told us of the captain yet.
395   When that is known and golden time convents,
         A solemn combination shall be made
         Of our dear souls.— Meantime, sweet sister,
         We will not part from hence.— Cesario, come —
         For so you shall be, while you are a man.
400   But when in other habits you are seen,
         Orsino's mistress and his fancy's queen.
                              Exeunt [*all, except Feste*]

FESTE   *Sings*
              When that I was and a little tiny boy,
              With hey, ho, the wind and the rain,
              A foolish thing was but a toy,
405   For the rain it raineth every day.

              But when I came to man's estate,
              With hey, ho, etc.
              Gainst knaves and thieves men shut their gate,
              For the rain, etc.

410   But when I came, alas! to wive,
              With hey, ho, etc.
              By swaggering could I never thrive,
              For the rain, etc.

---

383 **baffled** tricked/disgraced   386 **interlude** short play   390 **whirligig** spinning top/roundabout
395 **golden** auspicious   **convents** comes together/calls us   396 **combination** union   398 **hence** here,
i.e. Olivia's house   400 **habits** clothing   401 **fancy's** love's   402 **and a** a very   404 **foolish** trivial/silly
(may play on the sense of 'lewd')   **thing** may play on the sense of 'penis'   **toy** trifle/useless/fun (may play
on a sense of 'penis')   406 **man's estate** manhood   407 **etc.** indicates repeat of chorus   410 **wive**
marry   412 **swaggering** bullying/quarrelling

But when I came unto my beds,
With hey, ho, etc.
With toss-pots still had drunken heads,
For the rain, etc.

A great while ago the world begun,
With hey, ho, etc.
But that's all one, our play is done,
And we'll strive to please you every day. [*Exit*]

414 beds drunk to bed/old age   **416 With toss-pots** like other drunkards

TEXTUAL NOTES

F = First Folio text of 1623, the only authority for the play
F2 = a correction introduced in the Second Folio text of 1632
F3 = a correction introduced in the Third Folio text of 1663
Ed = a correction introduced by a later editor
SD = stage direction
SH = speech heading (i.e. speaker's name)

List of parts = Ed

1.1.1 SH ORSINO = Ed. F = *Duke*
1.2.15 Arion = Ed. F = *Orion*
1.3.95 curl by = Ed. F = coole my **97 me** = F2. F = we **does't** = Ed. F = dost **130 set** = Ed. F = sit **134 That's** = F3. F = That
1.5.5 SH FESTE = Ed. F = *Clo.* **164 SD *Viola*** = F2. F = *Violenta*
2.2.31 our = F2. F = O **32 made of** = Ed. F = made, if
2.3.2 *diluculo* *spelled Deliculo in* F **25 leman** = Ed. F = Lemon **132 a nayword** = Ed. F = an ayword
2.4.57 Fly away, fly = Ed. F = Fye away, fie **93 I** = Ed. F = It
2.5.110 staniel = Ed. F = stallion **138 born** = Ed. F = become **achieve** = F2. F = atcheeues **170 dear** = F2. F = deero
3.1.8 king = F2. F = Kings **66 wise men** = Ed. F = wisemens
3.2.7 thee the = F3. F = the
3.4.23 SH OLIVIA = F2. F = *Mal* **70 tang** = F2. F = langer
4.2.72 sport to = Ed. F = sport
5.1.208 pavin = F2. F = panyn **419 With hey** = F2. F = *hey*

SCENE-BY-SCENE ANALYSIS

ACT 1 SCENE 1

The play opens with music, a significant motif associated particularly with poetic expressions of love such as Orsino's opening speech. He describes the moment when his 'eyes did see Olivia first', introducing the themes of sight and perception. Valentine reports that Olivia refuses to hear Orsino's suit, as she is in seven years' mourning for her brother. She is 'veilèd', 'like a cloistress', introducing the motif of dress and associated themes of disguise, concealment and identity. Orsino reasons that if Olivia feels so much for a brother, she will feel even more for a lover.

ACT 1 SCENE 2

Viola, shipwrecked on the shores of Illyria, fears that her brother has been drowned. The Captain reassures her and tells her about Orsino's love for Olivia and how Olivia 'will admit no kind of suit'. While acknowledging that appearances can deceive, as 'nature with a beauteous wall / Doth oft close in pollution', Viola decides to trust the Captain. She asks him to help her disguise herself as a young man.

ACT 1 SCENE 3

Lines 1–100: Sir Toby Belch defends his intemperate behaviour but Maria tells him he should 'confine' himself 'within the modest limits of order', introducing a recurrent image which involves either literal confinement in clothes or rooms, or more metaphorical confinements of manners and social roles. Sir Toby's punning on 'confine' and Maria's responses set the comic tone for the exchanges amongst this set of characters, and reveal Maria's sharp wit. Maria scolds Sir Toby for his 'quaffing and drinking' and for bringing Sir Andrew Aguecheek to the house to woo Olivia, as 'he's a . . . fool'. Sir Andrew arrives and instantly proves her point; his foolishness makes him a figure of fun throughout the play.

Lines 101–136: Sir Andrew announces that he intends to leave because Olivia refuses to see him and he believes she'll accept Orsino's suit. Sir Toby encourages him not to go, arguing that Olivia will not 'match above her degree, neither in estate, years, nor wit', raising the question of social status. Sir Andrew agrees to stay 'a month longer' and confesses how much he enjoys 'masques and revels'. Sir Toby encourages him to 'caper', arguing that it is in their nature to do so being 'born under Taurus', thus raising another theme – fate and the influence of the stars.

ACT 1 SCENE 4

Viola, now disguised as 'Cesario', has become a favoured page of Orsino who singles him/her out to speak privately. In conventionally poetic language Orsino describes how he has 'unclasped' the 'book' of his 'secret soul' to Cesario/Viola, and sends him/her to court Olivia on his behalf. Cesario argues that he will not be admitted, but Orsino is confident that his youth will aid him and gives an ironically sensual description of the boy which reinforces the complicated nature of gender and sexual attraction explored throughout the play. He describes Cesario as so young he is almost feminine, with 'smooth and rubious' lips and a 'small pipe' for a voice, adding that Cesario's 'constellation' makes him right for the task. Although she agrees to go, Viola reveals in an aside another reason for her reluctance: she is in love with Orsino herself.

ACT 1 SCENE 5

Lines 1–164: Maria questions Feste about where he has been, saying that Olivia is displeased by his absence and will turn him away, but he refuses to say. Olivia arrives and Feste engages in 'good fooling', using the riddles and wordplay of his trade to please her and prevent her from throwing him out. Despite his role as 'clown', he is intelligent and perceptive: his fooling often contains reason and truth, as he says to Olivia 'I wear not motley in my brain', a reminder of the difference between appearance and identity. He wins Olivia round by suggesting that she is foolish to mourn for a brother whose soul is in heaven. Olivia comments that Feste improves but Malvolio cannot understand why she 'takes delight in such a barren rascal' and she accuses him of having 'a distempered appetite'. Maria reports that there is 'a fair young man' at the gate wishing to speak to Olivia, who sends Malvolio with instructions that, if the youth is from Orsino, she is 'sick, or not at home'. Sir Toby comes in, drunk, and Olivia instructs Feste to look after him; he comments that 'the fool shall look to the madman', one of many references to madness in the play, often as a parallel to love. Malvolio reports that the young man insists on speaking with Olivia, who relents but veils her face.

Lines 165–308: The encounter between the two women, one veiled and the other disguised, visually reinforces the themes of conceal-ment and identity, as does Viola's claim that 'I am not that I play'. Viola, as Cesario, begins to deliver Orsino's speech, commenting on how 'well penned' it is, thus emphasizing its contrived, conventional nature in comparison with her own passionate extemporized speeches later in the scene. She/he defeats Maria's attempts to throw her out and secures a private interview with Olivia, persuading her to show her face, praising her beauty but condemning her pride. She/he tells her that Orsino loves her 'With groans that thunder love, with sighs of fire'. Olivia acknowledges Orsino's good qualities: he is 'virtuous', 'noble' and 'gracious', but she 'cannot love him'. Olivia becomes more interested in the messenger, questioning him about his parentage, and encouraging him to come again. After Cesario leaves, it becomes clear that Olivia has fallen in love with 'him', creating a humorous situation of mistaken identity/gender and perhaps commenting on the shallow or arbitrary nature of romantic love. She sends Malvolio after the youth with a ring, pretending it was an unwanted gift from Orsino.

ACT 2 SCENE 1

Antonio has cared for Sebastian since rescuing him from 'the breach of the sea', but Sebastian decides he must now leave and refuses to allow Antonio to accompany him because the 'stars shine darkly' and are an evil influence over his fate. He reveals his true identity and talks of his twin sister, Viola, whom he believes is drowned. He describes her, placing particular emphasis on the likeness between them, thus establishing the potential for further complications and confused identities. Sebastian intends to go to 'Count Orsino's Court' and, despite having enemies there, Antonio decides to accompany him.

ACT 2 SCENE 2

Malvolio returns the ring to Cesario/Viola but she/he does not tell him the truth about it, realizing that Olivia has fallen in love with Cesario. She/he expresses sympathy, claiming that Olivia had 'better love a dream', and reiterating the illusory nature of her present identity. She emphasizes the unnatural state of affairs by describing her female–male identity as a 'poor monster' and summarizing the problem: as a man, her love for Orsino is hopeless, but as a woman, Olivia's love for her is 'thriftless'.

ACT 2 SCENE 3

Sir Toby and Sir Andrew are drinking late. Feste arrives and his quick-wittedness contrasts with Sir Andrew's genuine foolishness. Feste sings a wistful song that reflects some of the themes and events of the play. They begin singing a 'catch' together when Maria interrupts to tell them to be quiet or Olivia will send Malvolio to turn them out. Sir Toby responds with raucous popular songs when Malvolio appears and rebukes them for being drunk and noisy. He pompously tells Sir Toby that despite being Olivia's kinsman he will be thrown out if he does not behave. Sir Toby reminds Malvolio he is only a steward. Feste leaves and Malvolio accuses Maria of encouraging them by allowing them alcohol. After he has gone, Sir Andrew threatens to fight a duel with him but Maria claims she has a better plan: Malvolio is 'an affectioned ass' who aspires to high status and she will use this 'vice' against him. She plans to drop in his way a letter she has forged in Olivia's handwriting that will convince him his mistress is in love with him.

ACT 2 SCENE 4

Orsino, still indulging in his unrequited love, calls for music from Feste, who spends his time in both households. Orsino discusses love with Cesario/Viola, in a conversation that is fraught with ambiguity and dramatic irony, as Viola is forced to discuss love as though she were a man. She/he acknowledges that she/he is in love when prompted, but cannot say with whom. The conversation is charged with erotic undertones which again raises questions about gender, identity and the nature of attraction. Feste sings a melancholy love song and Orsino orders Cesario to plead once more with Olivia on his behalf. When Cesario suggests that Orsino should accept that Olivia does not love him, as a woman would have to whom Orsino was unable to love, he declares that there is a difference between men's and women's love. '[N]o woman's sides', he claims, 'Can bide the beating of so strong a passion'. Cesario relates how his 'father had a daughter loved a man', who concealed her love and, as a result, 'pined' with a 'green and yellow melancholy'. When Orsino asks if she 'died . . . of her love', he receives the ambiguous answer: 'I am all the daughters of my father's house, / And all the brothers too'.

ACT 2 SCENE 5

Sir Toby, Sir Andrew and Fabian conceal themselves in a 'box-tree' to watch Malvolio's response to the forged letter. Malvolio enters, imagining his future life as Count Malvolio, especially the power he would have over Sir Toby. The indignation of his concealed audience creates comedy, as does the dramatic irony of the situation. Malvolio finds the letter Maria has carefully prepared to trick him and recognizes 'Olivia's' handwriting. He painstakingly and vainly deduces that it is for/about him and that Olivia is in love with him. The letter urges him to wear yellow stockings and cross-garters, to spurn Sir Toby, and to smile continually in Olivia's presence as a sign of his love, all of which he resolves to do as he exits. The others come forward and Maria arrives, explaining that Olivia hates yellow stockings and cross-garters and is in no mood to be smiled at constantly. They go to watch the effects of the plan.

ACT 3 SCENE 1

Cesario/Viola arrives and, after a quick-witted exchange with Feste, gives him money. Sir Andrew admires Cesario's courtly language towards Olivia, who orders all the others to leave. Cesario continues to plead for Orsino but Olivia confesses it is Cesario she loves. She/he responds with pity, swearing that 'no woman' will ever be mistress of her heart.

ACT 3 SCENE 2

Sir Andrew is leaving since Olivia shows 'more favours to the count's servingman' than she does to him. Fabian argues that Olivia intends to make him jealous and wake his 'dormouse valour'. He claims Sir Andrew has missed an opportunity, and Sir Toby, keen for him to stay so he can continue to spend his money, suggests challenging Cesario to a duel. He instructs Sir Andrew to write a letter with 'gall enough in thy ink', emphasizing the difference between crafted words and reality. Maria calls them to have a look at Malvolio, who is obeying 'every point of the letter'.

ACT 3 SCENE 3

Antonio's strong attachment to Sebastian becomes more apparent as he addresses him in potentially homoerotic terms, expressing his 'desire' and 'willing love', furthering the play's exploration of the possibilities and complexities of same-gender love hinted at in Orsino's language to Cesario. Sebastian intends to explore Illyria but Antonio cannot accompany him because of Orsino's enmity. Instead, he gives Sebastian his purse and arranges to meet him later at an inn.

ACT 3 SCENE 4

The fast pace of this scene emphasizes the confusion of the various deceptions that are underway.

Lines 1–83: Olivia muses how best to woo Cesario then asks Maria to fetch Malvolio – such a 'sad and civil' person will suit her mood. Maria replies that he seems to have gone mad and 'does nothing but smile' but goes to call him. Olivia observes that she herself is mad, again drawing a parallel between love and madness. There is dramatic irony in the exchange between Olivia and Malvolio as he quotes lines from the letter he believes is from her. Olivia thinks he must be mad indeed and suggests he goes to bed, which he takes to be an invitation. Cesario's return is announced and Olivia leaves, instructing Maria to ask Sir Toby to look after Malvolio. Determined to read all events as evidence of Olivia's love, Malvolio recalls that the letter instructed him to 'be opposite with a kinsman' and decides that she has called for Sir Toby as a test.

Lines 84–197: Sir Toby, Fabian and Maria pretend to believe that Malvolio is mad and treat him accordingly until he exits in anger. They are delighted by the results of the plan and, in a moment of meta-theatrical awareness, Fabian declares that if he saw the scene 'played upon a stage', he would 'condemn it as an improbable fiction'. Sir Toby decides they should lock Malvolio in a darkened room, a traditional treatment for madness. Sir Andrew arrives with his challenge to Cesario. Sir Toby reads it and Fabian pretends to approve while revealing the nonsensical nature of the letter and the foolishness of its writer. They encourage Sir Andrew to look for Cesario in the orchard. When he has gone, Sir Toby comments that the challenge will 'breed no terror in the youth. He will find it comes from a clodpole', so instead of delivering it he will act as a go-between, inciting them against each other.

Lines 199–270: Olivia continues to woo Cesario/Viola, who displays a 'heart of stone' and continues to plead for Orsino. When Olivia has gone, Sir Toby and Fabian accost Cesario and pretend that he has enraged Sir Andrew, who is waiting for him in the orchard, 'bloody as the hunter'. Bewildered, Cesario claims that he has no quarrel with anyone, but they pretend that he must have done something to upset him, describing Sir Andrew's fury and his history as 'a devil in private brawl' who has killed three men. Alarmed, Cesario insists that he is no fighter and asks Sir Toby to speak to Sir Andrew on his behalf.

Lines 271–305: Sir Toby now describes Cesario's anger to Sir Andrew, who regrets challenging him. Sir Toby's aside reveals the pleasure he takes in making a fool of Sir Andrew. Fabian brings Cesario, and Sir Toby assures the two 'rivals' that the other insists on fighting but has promised not to draw blood.

Lines 306–396: Antonio arrives and, mistaking Cesario for Sebastian, offers to fight on his behalf. Sir Toby draws his sword on Antonio but they are interrupted by the officers who arrest Antonio for his previous offences against Orsino. Turning to Cesario, whom he takes to be Sebastian, he asks for his purse. Confused, Cesario denies all knowledge of it but offers Antonio half of his 'coffer'. Antonio is heartbroken by his friend's betrayal, claiming 'Thou hast, good Sebastian, done good feature shame', before being taken off to prison. Viola realizes that Sebastian may still be alive and rushes off to find him, followed by Sir Andrew who thinks that Cesario is running away from the duel.

ACT 4 SCENE 1

Feste, believing Sebastian to be Cesario, is trying to get him to go to Olivia and becoming increasingly angry at Sebastian's claims not to know him. Sir Andrew arrives and, mistaking Sebastian for Cesario, strikes him. Sebastian retaliates and he and Sir Toby draw upon each other as Olivia enters. She orders Sir Toby to 'hold' and 'be gone', which he does, accompanied by Sir Andrew and Fabian. Olivia begs 'dear Cesario' to 'Be not offended' and asks him to accompany her back to the house to be told of Sir Toby's many faults and to learn to 'smile at this'. Sebastian questions whether he is 'mad' or whether it is 'a dream' – both repeated images of love in the play – as he willingly submits to Olivia's request.

ACT 4 SCENE 2

Maria helps Feste to disguise himself as 'Sir Topas the curate' and he asks 'what is "that" but "that" and "is" but "is"?' – an ironic question given that very little within the play 'is' 'that' which it seems to be. Sir Toby takes him to see Malvolio who is locked up. Malvolio begs the 'priest' to believe he is not mad, but Feste toys cruelly with him: when Malvolio says that he is in 'hideous darkness', Feste tells him that he is in a room full of windows and must be mad. Sir Toby then tells Feste to speak to Malvolio as himself to see if the joke might be ended without trouble as he fears Olivia's reaction. Feste then converses with Malvolio as himself and as 'Sir Topas', increasing the confusion of his identity. He agrees to bring light, ink and paper so that Malvolio can write to Olivia.

ACT 4 SCENE 3

Bewildered, Sebastian wonders whether he 'Or else the lady's mad', as he contemplates Olivia's love for him. He wonders where Antonio is as he would like to discuss the situation with him, but when Olivia arrives with a priest he agrees to marry her.

ACT 5 SCENE 1

Lines 1–96: Fabian wants to read Malvolio's letter, but Feste refuses to let him. Orsino and Cesario ask for Olivia and Feste goes to fetch her. Antonio is brought in by the officers. Cesario tells Orsino that this is the man who rescued him from the duel and the officers explain that it is 'that Antonio / That took the *Phoenix*'. Orsino asks what foolish boldness has brought a 'Notable pirate' to Illyria. Antonio claims that he 'never yet was thief or pirate' and explains that he was drawn there by 'witchcraft', enchanted by Sebastian, whom he believes to be standing next to Orsino. He calls Cesario a 'most ingrateful boy' and accuses him of 'false cunning'. Orsino and Cesario are confused, explaining that Cesario has been in Illyria for the last three months.

Lines 97–155: Olivia arrives and demands to speak to Cesario, believing that she has just married him in secret. Orsino tries to woo her but she flatly rejects his suit and refuses to listen to any more of his wooing, claiming that it is as 'fat and fulsome' to her ear 'As howling after music'. Stung, Orsino threatens to kill Cesario despite the fact that he, too, cares deeply for him. Cesario declares that he would die for Orsino because he loves him, at which point Olivia cries, 'Cesario, husband, stay.' Cesario denies any knowledge of their 'marriage'.

Lines 156–215: The priest arrives and, believing Cesario to be Sebastian, confirms that he is married to Olivia. As Cesario protests, Sir Andrew arrives calling for a surgeon as 'the count's gentleman, one Cesario' has broken his head and 'given Sir Toby a bloody coxcomb too'. Cesario denies this as well and Sir Toby arrives, very drunk. As Olivia orders Sir Toby and Sir Andrew to be removed, Sebastian appears.

Lines 216–324: Sebastian, not seeing Viola, apologizes to Olivia for injuring her kinsman. Everyone is astonished by the likeness between Cesario and the newcomer, who is delighted to see Antonio. Finally, Sebastian notices Cesario and, astounded by their likeness, demands to know his name and parentage. After mutual questioning, Viola reveals her true identity and Sebastian points out that Olivia 'would have been contracted to a maid'. Orsino reminds Viola of the number of times she has said that she loves him and asks to see her in her 'woman's weeds', which are with the Captain, whom Malvolio has had arrested. Olivia still believes Malvolio to be mad but Fabian reads his letter and Orsino comments that it 'savours not much of distraction'. Olivia sends Fabian to fetch Malvolio.

Lines 325–421: Olivia and Orsino make peace and she offers to host the double wedding celebration at her house. He agrees and releases his 'page' from service, saying that she is to become instead her 'master's mistress', which reinforces the gender confusions of the play, particularly as he continues to call her 'Cesario'. Fabian brings Malvolio, who shows Olivia the letter and asks why she has treated him so badly. Olivia recognizes the writing as Maria's and Fabian confesses to the plot and explains the reasons behind it, adding that Sir Toby has married Maria as a reward for her wit. Malvolio swears to be revenged 'on the whole pack of you', and although Orsino tells Fabian to entreat him to peace, this strikes a discordant note, as does the impossibility of a conclusion to Antonio's love for Sebastian, forgotten as everyone leaves for the 'solemn combination' of their 'dear souls', a symbol of the restored order. The play concludes with a wistful song from Feste.

TWELFTH NIGHT IN PERFORMANCE: THE RSC AND BEYOND

The best way to understand a Shakespeare play is to see it or ideally to participate in it. By examining a range of productions, we may gain a sense of the extraordinary variety of approaches and interpretations that are possible – a variety that gives Shakespeare his unique capacity to be reinvented and made 'our contemporary' four centuries after his death.

We begin with a brief overview of the play's theatrical and cinematic life, offering historical perspectives on how it has been performed. We then analyse in more detail a series of productions staged over the last half-century by the Royal Shakespeare Company. The sense of dialogue between productions that can only occur when a company is dedicated to the revival and investigation of the Shakespeare canon over a long period, together with the uniquely comprehensive archival resource of promptbooks, programme notes, reviews and interviews held on behalf of the RSC at the Shakespeare Birthplace Trust in Stratford-upon-Avon, allows an 'RSC stage history' to become a crucible in which the chemistry of the play can be explored.

Finally, we go to the horse's mouth. Modern theatre is dominated by the figure of the director, who must hold together the whole play, whereas the actor must concentrate on his or her part. The director's viewpoint is therefore especially valuable. Shakespeare's plasticity is wonderfully revealed when we hear directors of highly successful productions answering the same questions in very different ways.

FOUR CENTURIES OF *TWELFTH NIGHT*: AN OVERVIEW

The first recorded performance of *Twelfth Night* was at London's Middle Temple on 2 February (Candlemas) 1602. The student barrister, John Manningham, noted:

> At our feast we had a play called *Twelve Night, or What You Will*, much like *The Comedy of Errors* or *Menaechmi* in Plautus but most like and near to that in Italian called *Inganni*. A good practice in it to make the steward believe his lady widow was in love with him, by counterfeiting a letter as from his lady, in general terms telling him what she liked best in him, and prescribing his gesture in smiling, his apparel, etc., and then when he came to practise, making believe they took him to be mad.[1]

Despite Manningham's confusion over details, the play was certainly Shakespeare's *Twelfth Night* performed by the Lord Chamberlain's (later King's) Men, probably with Shakespeare himself among the cast. It is generally assumed that Robert Armin, the company clown known for his singing and musical abilities, would have played Feste, with the notoriously thin John Sincklo as Sir Andrew Aguecheek.

The play was probably written in 1601; it has been suggested that it may have been written for and first performed at court on Twelfth Night (6 January) 1601 before Elizabeth I and her guest, Virginio Orsino, Duke of Bracciano.[2] It was later performed before James I on Easter Monday 1618 and again at Candlemas in 1623 when it was simply called *Malvolio*. Charles I wrote this alternative title in his own Folio edition of Shakespeare's plays. The character's popularity is attested in Leonard Digges' 1640 commendatory verse to the first edition of Shakespeare's collected poems:

> . . . Let but Beatrice
> And Benedick be seen, lo, in a trice
> The Cockpit galleries, boxes, all are full
> To hear Malvolio, that cross-gartered gull.[3]

After the Restoration of the monarchy in 1660 and the reopening of the theatres, which were closed during the civil war and Interregnum (1642–60), Shakespeare's plays were divided up between the two licensed companies. Major innovations in performance style were introduced with movable scenery, creating a more visual, illusionist theatre, and the presence of women onstage. *Twelfth Night* was assigned to William d'Avenant's Duke of York's Men. Shakespeare's comedies did not suit the taste of the new age though. Samuel Pepys saw three productions of *Twelfth Night* between 1661 and 1669, none of which he enjoyed, even though the leading actor of the age, Thomas Betterton, played Sir Toby Belch. Indeed, Pepys thought it 'one of the weakest plays that ever I saw on the stage'.[4] In 1703 William Burnaby produced *Love Betray'd, or, The Agreeable Disappointment*, an adaptation which retained only around sixty of Shakespeare's lines but failed in its attempt to update the play to suit contemporary tastes. 'More radical transformations, such as William Wycherley's *The Plain Dealer* or Pierre Marivaux's *The False Servant*', which used Shakespeare's play as source material, were more successful.[5]

It was not until David Garrick's production at the Theatre Royal in 1741 with Charles Macklin as Malvolio, Hannah Pritchard as Viola and Kitty Clive as Olivia that Shakespeare's *Twelfth Night* enjoyed popularity and success once more. Macklin's casting as Malvolio thrust the character into prominence, as the earliest productions had done. As with his Shylock in Shakespeare's *Merchant of Venice*, Macklin's psychological interpretation altered the perception of both characters bringing out the pathos of the roles, making them more sympathetic, even 'quasi-tragic figures'.[6] This effect was subsequently intensified in Robert Bensley's performance in John Philip Kemble's production, of which Charles Lamb wrote, 'I confess, that I never saw the catastrophe of this character, while Bensley played it, without a kind of tragic interest.'[7] Kemble's 1811 production was the first to reverse the order of the first two scenes of the play – a strategy since adopted by numerous directors.

In the early nineteenth century emphasis was given to the play's musical and spectacular potential. Frederic Reynolds presented an operatic adaptation at Covent Garden in 1820 incorporating the masque from *The Tempest* as well as extracts from Shakespeare's sonnets and his narrative poem *Venus and Adonis*. At the same time, 'breeches' roles such as Viola, in which women pretended to be men, with their transgressive potential for assuming figure-revealing masculine attire, became extremely popular. The American actress Charlotte Cushman, best known for her performance as Romeo to her sister's Juliet, played Viola in New York with her sister Susan as Olivia. The production transferred to London's Haymarket Theatre in 1846. Samuel Phelps' productions at Sadler's Wells in 1847 and 1858 transformed Malvolio curiously into a Spanish Golden Age *hidalgo*, one nobly born but poor (Don Quixote is the most famous literary example of the type).

Charles Kean presented a typically lavish pictorial staging with his wife, Ellen Tree, as Viola in 1850. Five years later Kate Terry starred in Alfred Wigan's production at the St James' Theatre in which, with some rearrangement of the text, she played both Viola and Sebastian. Kean's spectacular set was matched by Henry Irving's in 1884:

> The Lyceum Illyria is a land where ornate palaces with their cool balconies and colonnades and their mazy arabesque traceries, look forth among groves of palms, and plantains, and orange trees, and cedars, over halcyon seas dotted with bird-like feluccas and high-prowed fishing boats.[8]

While Ellen Terry was praised for her Viola, critics were divided by Irving's Malvolio. A number objected to his mannered delivery, 'When an absence of humorous expression is required to give a speech its full comic effect, Mr Irving's restless eyebrows and obliquely twinkling eyes do him a disservice.' The production's 'tone of serious tragedy', which culminated in his collapsing into 'a nerveless state of prostrate dejection . . . stretched on the straw of a dungeon worthy of *Fidelio*', was felt to unbalance the play: 'There can be no doubt that the straw which clung to Mr Irving's dress from the mad-house scene was the last straw which broke the patience of a certain section of the first night audience.'[9]

Augustin Daly's 1893 production, which featured a violent storm as well as a moonlit rose garden, cut and rearranged the text drastically. It was generally well-received, though, both in New York and London when it transferred the following year. In the words of the critic William Archer, it had 'the one supreme merit which, in a Shakespearean revival, covers a multitude of sins – it really "revives" the play, makes it live again'.[10] For George Bernard Shaw, Ada Rehan's Viola was the production's only redeeming feature: 'the moment she strikes up the true Shakespearian music, and feels her way to her part altogether by her sense of that music, the play returns to life and all the magic is there'.[11] Shaw deplored the liberties Daly had taken with the text, though, which included cutting the 'dark-house' scene in Act 4 when Malvolio is imprisoned and taunted with madness.

Surprisingly, William Poel also cut this scene in his experimental production at the Middle Temple in 1897 in the (reconstructed) hall where Manningham had seen the Chamberlain's Men perform it. Keen to gauge its possibilities as a playing space, Poel's Elizabethan Stage Society employed original staging practices as far as possible. Herbert Beerbohm Tree cut the same scene in his production at the Haymarket in 1901. George Odell described it as

> the most extraordinary single setting I have ever beheld. It was the garden of Olivia, extending terrace by terrace to the extreme back of the stage, with very real grass, real fountains, paths and descending steps. I never saw anything approaching it for beauty and *vraisemblance*.[12]

Unfortunately the set's complexity made it impossible to strike so that a number of completely inappropriate scenes had to be played on it. Tree himself played Malvolio, emphasizing comedy rather than pathos as the 'peacock-like' steward was always followed by 'four smaller Malvolios in the production who aped the large one in dress and deportment'.[13]

Essentially an ensemble piece with the lines distributed more-or-less evenly across the major roles, twentieth-century productions generally eschewed the earlier practice of building up a star part.

Harley Granville-Barker's 'legendary'[14] 1912 production at the Savoy Theatre, influenced by the ideas and practices of Poel, has proved of lasting significance in thinking about the play. Michael Billington records how

> Norman Wilkinson's black-and-silver setting, evoking a half-Italianised Elizabethan court, combined beauty with intimacy: there was a formal garden with a great staircase right and left, with drop curtains and a small inner tapestry set for the carousal. The verse was spoken with lightness, speed, and dexterity... above all, Granville-Barker got rid of all the false accretions of stage tradition and sought for the essential truth of character.[15]

1. Harley Granville-Barker production, Savoy Theatre, 1912, the 'black and silver setting evoking a half Italianised Elizabethan court', depicting Henry Ainley as Malvolio, Arthur Whitby as Sir Toby, Leah Bateman Hunter as Maria, Hayden Coffin as Feste and Leon Quartermaine as Sir Andrew.

Lillah McCarthy's Viola was praised as was Arthur Whitby's Sir Toby. Henry Ainley played Malvolio as a 'Puritan prig', while one of the chief innovations was the casting of the middle-aged Hayden Coffin as Feste, whom Barker saw as 'not a young man', adding: 'There runs through all he says and does that vein of irony through which we may so often mark one of life's self-acknowledge failures.'[16]

Barker himself admired the French-language version by Jacques Copeau first staged in 1914 at the Théâtre du Vieux-Colombier. He reviewed the 1921 revival favourably, noting with approval the 'precision, variety, clarity and, above all, passion' of the actors' diction.[17] There were several revivals in the 1930s and 1940s. Edith Evans played Viola in Harcourt Williams' 1932 production at the Old Vic. Five years later, again at the Old Vic, Tyrone Guthrie directed Laurence Olivier as Sir Toby, Alec Guinness as Sir Andrew and Marius Goring as Feste, with Jessica Tandy playing both Viola and Sebastian. Jacques Copeau's nephew, Michel Saint-Denis, staged the play at the Phoenix in 1938 with Peggy Ashcroft as a remarkable Viola, a production that was subsequently filmed for the BBC. In Margaret Webster's 1940–41 Theatre Guild production at New York's St James' Theater the Jacobean masque provided inspiration for set and costumes. Helen Hayes' Viola was warmly praised, although opinions were divided about Maurice Evans' Malvolio, played as 'a Cockney, a head butler raised to sublimation'.[18]

Hugh Hunt's 1950 Old Vic revival owed much to the Italian *commedia dell'arte* – both 'arty *and* hearty': 'Its best bits are the hearty bits, centred around a fine scarlet-faced, broad-bottomed, big-bellied, rasping Roger Livesey as Sir Toby. Its worst bits are the arty framework which the producer has thought fit to provide.'[19] Peggy Ashcroft playing Viola was singled out for praise:

> It is long since I have seen a Viola so fitted to the play. Peggy Ashcroft is never brisk or pert, never self-consciously disguised ...She is very quiet, very loyal. She does not juggle with words ... this Viola realises what love can be – she is not toying with it – and the 'willow cabin' speech comes from her with an absolute sincerity, with no kind of elaborate preparation ... And

this is not Peggy Ashcroft's finest moment: that comes at the very end, when Viola, her lost brother before her, answers his question, 'What countryman? What name? What parentage?' with the barely-breathed 'Of Messaline.' Now the play is played. Viola has her reward at last in the strange bittersweet Illyrian world. The Old Vic can be happy indeed to have had such a performance as this at its opening.[20]

Sir John Gielgud's production at the Shakespeare Memorial Theatre in 1955 with Laurence Olivier as Malvolio, Vivien Leigh as Viola, Paul Daneman as Feste, Maxine Audley as Olivia and Richard Burton as Sir Toby had been eagerly anticipated. Despite the beauty of the set and Elizabethan costumes and its star cast, Gielgud himself acknowledged that 'Somehow the production did not work.'[21] The critic Peter Fleming suggested: 'There is a certain lack of heart about this elegant and well-paced production': Vivien Leigh's Viola, though 'trim, pretty, poised and resourceful', had a quality of 'non-involvement'. Likewise, Olivier's 'brilliant and deeply-considered study of Malvolio' possessed some 'inner quality of reserve or detachment'.[22] Billington concluded that 'If one had to sum up his performance in a word it would be "camp".'[23]

Tyrone Guthrie's production at the Stratford Festival Ontario in 1957 was more successful in integrating the play's diverse elements. Siobhan McKenna's Viola won especial praise:

With economical grace and shining eye she creates Illyria out of bare boards as divinely as if she had a vision of Heaven . . . With the security of Miss McKenna's power, Dr Guthrie feels free to play his clowns as less silly than is the lamentable tradition. Sir Toby, Maria and Sir Andrew are well-defined characters.[24]

Against these,

Feste became a sad, ageing fool full of the pathos of his position where he is retained not for his wit but for his length of service. His melancholy, honestly come by, thus makes Malvolio's even more priggish, rendering his gulling and final turning-off not only poignant, which it always is, but even credible which it seldom is.[25]

Critics were initially confused by Peter Hall's 1958 production at the Shakespeare Memorial Theatre, now regarded as a classic of its time. John Wain saw it as 'a perfect example of how a Shakespeare play can be ripped apart by the twin steel claws of naturalism and gimmickry',[26] while Alan Brien, having criticized every aspect of the production, concluded: 'Mr Hall is wrong and I am right. And yet how I enjoyed every moment of his wrongness.'[27] Peter Jackson offered a more positive assessment of its innovative qualities:

> What a rib-tickling, refreshing *Twelfth Night* Peter Hall has conjured up...a production that is smooth and gay and brimming with new ways to play old tricks. Dorothy Tutin's golden Viola is wonderfully boyish, breathless and bewildered and always completely audible. She is alive, and to be alive in a cast like this means working double overtime. To force Olivia to play for laughs while surrounded on all sides by comedians with far better lines does not give the actress a fighting chance, but Geraldine McEwan, with her piping voice and plaintive little gestures, draws such sympathy from the audience that the approach is almost justified.[28]

Designed by the painter Lila de Nobili and set in the Caroline court pre-civil war, the production was described by the critic Robert Speaight as 'a rich symphony in russet'.[29] It was revived two years later for the Royal Shakespeare Company with a substantially revised cast (discussed in detail below, along with other RSC productions).

One of the most successful non-RSC productions of the late twentieth century was at Stratford Ontario in 1975, directed by David Jones, with Kathleen Widdoes as Viola and Brian Bedford as a puritanical Malvolio. For his 1980 production at the Circle Repertory Theatre, New York, David Mamet allowed the actors to choose their own costumes in accordance with their conception of their character. This resulted in a medley of costumes which divided critics, many of whom thought it an 'irresponsible gimmick', while others argued that it revealed 'a fine intuition into the play's heart'.[30] If critics were divided about costumes and several individual performances, they were unanimous in their praise for Lindsay Crouse's Viola.

In 1987 Kenneth Branagh directed the Renaissance Theatre Company's production at the Riverside Studios. It was set in a wintry landscape with a Christmas tree and a snowy cemetery. Richard Briers' 'first-rate' Malvolio was 'nicely balanced by Anton Lesser's shaggy-locked Feste, Frances Barber's clear-spoken Viola, and Caroline Langrishe's Olivia'.[31] The production was later re-created for television. In the same year Declan Donnellan's production for Cheek by Jowl played at the Donmar Warehouse after a lengthy provincial tour. It was a controversial and irreverent production, with the drunken revellers blasting out the Sinatra classic 'My Way'. Michael Ratcliffe in the *Observer* thought it 'a *Twelfth Night* for those who had never seen the play before and those who thought they never wanted to see it again', whereas Peter Kemp in the *Independent* argued that 'Self-indulgence – mocked in *Twelfth Night* – is pandered to in this production'.[32]

Tim Supple's 1998 production at the Young Vic contrived to be both 'visually simple, its costumes vaguely suggesting an Eastern exoticism, and aurally rich, the alien beauty of its Eastern melodies and instruments creating an Illyria of otherness and wonder'.[33] For his final season in 2002–03 at the Donmar Warehouse, Sam Mendes staged the play in repertory with Chekhov's *Uncle Vanya*. With Simon Russell Beale as Malvolio, Emily Watson as Viola and David Bradley as Aguecheek, it was 'a production that found multiple dimensions of *Twelfth Night* with highly suggestive staging and music and a minimum of detail'.[34]

Twelfth Night has been set everywhere and nowhere: in 2000 Shakespeare and Company set it 'against fragments of a deteriorating seaside carnival'; in the same year the Theatre at Monmouth's production was set in 'a 1920s seaside resort', while the Alabama Shakespeare Festival's production of that year created a '1930s cabaret mood'. On the other hand, companies such as the 'touring five-person troupe Actors From the London Stage, thrive on early modern practices such as open spaces and doubling, tripling, and quadrupling roles. In the 1994 performance . . . at the Clemson

Shakespeare Festival, Geoffrey Church played Orsino, Feste, and Fabian.'[35] Similarly, Shenandoah Shakespeare's productions in 1995 and 2000–01 successfully experimented with cross-gender cross-casting, with David McCallum playing both Maria and Sebastian. The 2002 all-male production at Shakespeare's Globe theatre in London played with the sexual ambiguity of the casting, causing the audience to gasp as Orsino kissed Cesario. Mark Rylance found a great deal of unsuspected comedy in the part of Olivia, and Paul Chahidi was a wonderfully busy Maria. The production was especially successful when played in the hall of the Middle Temple, where Manningham had seen the original version exactly four hundred years before.

The play has continued in recent years to thrive onstage despite Michael Billington's contention that while 'Twelfth Night may be Shakespeare's most perfect comedy, it is also one of the hardest to bring off in the theatre because of its sheer kaleidoscopic range of moods'.[36] The illusionist productions of the nineteenth century are a thing of the past, their place taken by film with all its potential for realism. There were a number of silent screen versions, including Charles Kent's for Vitagraph in 1910 which, despite lasting for only twelve minutes, employs relatively sophisticated cinematographic techniques.[37] In 1955 Yakov Fried produced a Russian-language version in black and white which critics have seen as a response to the death of Stalin in its 'fresh air of political renewal' which 'opens up Shakespeare's play into a world of expansive great houses and the rich, open landscape of faraway mountains, open fields, and the promise of unlimited vistas or reverberate hills'.[38]

In 1937 the BBC broadcast a live excerpt of the play, the first known instance of a work of Shakespeare being performed on television, which featured a young Greer Garson. A 1939 television production of the entire play directed by Michel Saint-Denis starred Peggy Ashcroft as Viola and George Devine as Sir Toby. In 1970 John Dexter and John Sichel produced a version for television with Ralph Richardson as Sir Toby, Alec Guinness as Malvolio and Tommy Steele as a youthful Feste, with Joan Plowright playing both Viola and Sebastian. Two years later Ron Wertheim's Playboy production was made: 'As one might expect, the language of the play is ruthlessly cut to accommodate numerous and oddly innocent examples of Illyrian erotic revelry, rich in nudity, pastoral landscapes, soft-focus camerawork, and slow motion.'[39] The BBC's 1980 version is generally regarded as more successful, 'graced with spirited performances by Felicity Kendall as Viola and Sinead Cusack as Olivia', with Alec McCowen as Malvolio and Robert Hardy as Sir Toby. It nevertheless 'still suffered to some extent under the weight of canonical seriousness', and Ford notes: 'There was a strange echo of the detailed, illusionistic settings of Beerbohm Tree.'[40]

Trevor Nunn, who surprisingly had never directed the play on stage in his distinguished theatrical career, directed a successful film version in 1996. It was set in the nineteenth century and boasted a star-studded cast, with Imogen Stubbs as Viola, Helena Bonham-Carter as Olivia, Toby Stephens as Orsino, Mel Smith as Sir Toby, Richard E. Grant as Sir Andrew, Ben Kingsley as Feste, Imelda Staunton as Maria and Nigel Hawthorne as Malvolio. The film opens by 'inventing a kind of mock prologue that depicts the sinking of the ship and the rescue of Viola'.[41] Ford argues that 'Nunn's emphasis on song and music . . . allow his film to capture some of the aural energies of the play without compromising the film.' Nunn successfully exploits filmic technique: 'In one wonderful moment early in the film, Nunn uses the camera to capture the complex energies swirling within Viola. We see her in disguise, walking along the sea, determined to master her manly walk in a state of mind both resourceful and ironic.'[42]

There were ironic references to *Twelfth Night* in John Madden's 1998 film *Shakespeare in Love* in which Gwyneth Paltrow played a young noblewoman called Viola who disguises herself as a boy in order to become an actor. In 2003 Tim Supple directed an updated version for television with Parminder Nagra as Viola, David Troughton as Sir Toby, Chiwetel Ejiofor as Orsino and Michael Maloney as Malvolio. A Channel 4 documentary charted the course of production – *21st Century Bard: The Making of Twelfth Night*. In 2006 a contemporary teenage update called *She's the Man*, directed by Andy Fickman and starring Amanda Hynes, set the play in a prep school called Illyria.

AT THE RSC

Laughter in Illyria?

Twelfth Night is often referred to as Shakespeare's most melancholy or darkest comedy, and surely unrequited love and grief are not what you'd instantly think of as the basis for laughter. Nevertheless, the most painful of emotions are often the catalyst for the most beautiful of poetry. Writing about tragedy, Shelley believed, 'The pleasure that is in sorrow is sweeter than the pleasure of pleasure itself.'[43] Shakespeare's genius in *Twelfth Night* is to take the pleasure that we feel from tragedy and successfully combine it with farce to create a hauntingly bittersweet comedy. The effect on the audience is to have them on the verge of tears or laughter at any given moment. In doing so he has created the most potent mixture of pleasures derived from the light and dark sides of literature.

The director of a production of *Twelfth Night* has to make decisions about whether his or her production will attempt to balance the elements of light and dark in the play, or to go to one extreme or the other. Productions by the RSC demonstrate a wide variety of approaches, and the difficulty in succeeding with this emotionally complex play is shown in its reviews. Directors have invariably been criticized for omitting comedy, neglecting depth of emotion, or failing to find a balance between the two.

From the 1960s onwards a definite shift took place in which the darker elements became the central focus – aspects such as the treatment of madness, sexuality, and the character of Feste were radically re-examined, altering the tone of the play:

> *Twelfth Night* is widely accepted as a supreme harmonizing of the romantic and the comic, sweet and the astringent. The admirable production, then, is held to be one which holds these elements in balance. It is in the inflection which a production gives to *Twelfth Night* that the special interest lies. And this inflection has undoubtedly modulated in recent years. Broadly, and crudely: *Twelfth Night* used to be funny, and is now much less so. What has happened?[44]

John Barton's 1969 staging is widely considered a landmark production because it was markedly different in tone from previous productions. His exploration of the psychological complexity of the characters created for one critic 'the most austere *Twelfth Night* I have seen';[45] for another it was suffused with 'a kind of wintry melancholy'.[46] The programme notes pointed to this darker reading:

> For some characters [Orsino, Viola, Olivia and Sebastian] ... holiday perpetuates itself ... The other characters of the comedy, by contrast, are exiled into reality. For most of them, holiday is paid for in ways that have real life consequences ... None of these characters can be absorbed into the harmony of the romantic plot. For the rest of us ... the play is done and we return to normality along with Sir Toby, Aguecheek and Malvolio ... we have been dismissed to a world beyond holiday, where 'the rain it raineth every day'.[47]

Barton's production effectively used the sound of the sea to bring in what Matthew Arnold in his great Victorian poem of loss, 'Dover Beach', called 'the eternal note of sadness':

> The audience takes its seats to find Richard Pasco's Orsino listening to his musicians. Presently an aural disturbance comes upon the music. It grows louder, and is identified as the sound of the sea crashing upon the shore.[48]

> Thus Orsino's longing for love is overlaid with the storm that heralds Viola's arrival, prompting, through the use of sound, the idea that she will awaken him from romantic delusion to reality and true love. The sound recurred during Viola's conversation with Orsino in Act 2 scene 4 and during her reunion with Sebastian.[49]

Viola acts as a catalyst, a storm of honest emotion: 'throughout the play, the sea still tosses its waves: there are moments when the setting reminded me of the tunnel of a dream, a journeying place of the mind'.[50]

Critic Robert Speaight experienced a sense of 'the howling of the gale outside the gilded cage of Orsino's palace; reality at odds with romanticism'.[51] Even the comic characters were serious: 'The knightly revels are sad too. Barrie Ingham's Sir Andrew is a knight of woeful countenance':[52]

> Most startling and persuasive of the group is Elizabeth Spriggs Maria: no longer the usual bundle of fun, but a prim Edinburgh housekeeper in gold rimmed spectacles, besotted with Sir Toby and only mounting the Malvolio intrigue with the purpose of luring him into marriage . . . the essence of the reading appears after the carousel scene where she steals back hoping to catch Sir Toby alone, only to be packed off blubbering by the selfish old brute ('It is too late to go to bed') . . . Malvolio: the agent of so much fear in the household, and finally the most wounded member of all – broken double under the weight of his humiliation, [stumbled] off stage after handing Olivia his chain of office. It is not a happy household.[53]

In John Caird's 1983 production inherent melancholy resulted from the pain of love. The programme, instead of the usual notes, was littered with Shakespeare's sonnets on unrequited and barren love: 'Set in the Jacobean period, the production accentuated a sense of decay and confinement by employing a ruined garden, rusting gates, and a mortuary chapel as components of the set design.'[54] Thunder rumbled in the background only achieving downpour at the end of the play, cued by Feste's song. The impact of frustrated love and thoughts of mortality on Viola's psyche was demonstrated by an inspired bit of acting from Zoë Wanamaker:

> the decisive moment in [her] performance as Viola came when reunited with Sebastian, she showed her deep fear that her drowned brother had returned as a ghost to frighten her. She had suffered enough already, and now, on top of everything, the spirit world was playing an unforgivable trick, trifling inexcusably with her deepest feelings of loss and grief.[55]

In recent years there has been a definite reaction against the 'twentieth-century preoccupation with the play's melancholy'.[56]

Ian Judge's 1994 production played 'the broad comedy to the hilt'.[57] When discussing the play he observed that:

> The beginning of *Twelfth Night* deals with bereavement: we see a girl hopelessly distressed, having lost her brother but then, because of hope and friendship she is able to re-invent herself: a disguise allows her to create a new life. That's comedy, not because it's funny, but because hope and joy can be seen to spring from happiness. *Twelfth Night* also shows the comedy of falling in love, which occurs when people turn themselves inside out and almost reach the edge of madness. There are a thousand different ways of laughing and I think that *Twelfth Night* touches them all.[58]

Taking a more extreme approach to the comic aspects, Adrian Noble's 1997 production had an exaggerated and comic non-realist feel to the characters, setting and costumes: 'When there are gags to be gone for, Noble goes for them, adopting the anarchic visual humour of pantomime.'[59] The set, with brash, bold primary colours, was reminiscent of a child's play-box:

> a pop-art playground complete with jokey lurid green carpet for the garden box-hedge. It's overhung by a day-glo blue arc, on top of which sits an orb that travels a day's length from west to east and sun to moon during the play's course.[60]

> The design ... often seemed to take the 1950s (perhaps as perceived through *Carry On* films) as its historical cue ... the production was, in short, bold, brash and cartoon-like.[61]

Michael Billington referred to it as 'a kind of pop-art Alice in Illyria with little emotional reality or erotic tension'.[62] Although entertaining, it annoyed critics with its gimmickries. Also, by playing up the comic aspects, Noble lost the poetry of the play. Dimension and depth were lost in the interpretation of the characters. The programme notes reduced them to types found in an enneagram report,[*] and illustrated them with exaggerated and grotesque caricatures:

> *Twelfth Night* is the darkest and most haunting of Shakespeare's great comedies, its humour constantly shadowed by cruelty and

---

[*] Ancient personality test based on nine psycho-spiritual types.

a keen awareness of mortality. Here, however the poetry is almost entirely missing and you are left with little more than crude, one-dimensional farce.[63]

Noble's production was a reaction against the type of *Twelfth Night* that had emerged since the 1960s, a conscious lampooning of the Chekhovian take on the play which began with John Barton's production in 1969. The effect of treating the characters as purely comic creations, however, was revealing in the failure of these productions to make you *feel*. It appears that the comedy, inherent in Shakespeare's text, comes from the characters themselves and is most effective when actors play the characters straight. Judi Dench, who played Viola 1969, remarked: 'John Barton was the one who said it's such a bittersweet play, that if you do that [i.e. play it purely for comedy] it tips over. It's not pure comedy.'[64] As academic and theatre historian Ralph Berry explains,

> a taste for dark comedy has long been prevalent ... the entire network of assumptions sustaining the old *Twelfth Night* has collapsed. And that raises the whole question of what is called, for want of a better word, comedy ... A modern production of *Twelfth Night* is obliged to redefine comedy, knowing always that its ultimate event is the destruction of a notably charmless bureaucrat.[65]

But, he goes on to ask, 'Do we laugh at it?'

'Are All the People Mad?'

> There is a great deal in *Twelfth Night* about madness ... for all its comedy and charm, [it is] very much darker than that. Like so many of Shakespeare's plays, it's about what happens to individuals when their idea of themselves prevents them from taking in the reality of the world around them. They act irrationally, lose their sense of proportion, become – in a way – unbalanced.[66]

Orsino is a victim of a type of madness to which the most admirable characters are sometimes subject. Its usual causes are boredom, lack of physical love, and excessive imagination, and the victim is unaware that he is in love with love rather than with a person.[67]

Orsino's complete lack of reason with regards to Olivia's refusal of him has been emphasized in more recent years. Michael Boyd's 2005 production had him in various states of disarray and undress, in a half-waking, half-sleeping state, indulging his every 'romantic' whim, at the expense of his personal musicians, who had to get up and play music whenever he dictated. At one point they appear in dressing gowns, obviously dragged out of bed to perpetuate his obsessive sickness. Clearly unbalanced at the start of the play, his fantasy became so overwhelming that, in the final scene, he threatened to murder both Olivia and Viola. The question of whether or not he had regained his sanity remained ambiguous.

This emphasis on the madness of Orsino's wooing threw light on the fact that his behaviour and romantic posturing is as forced as that of Malvolios. Faced with Viola/Cesario, who expresses her true feelings for Orsino through her entreaties, Olivia is awoken by a genuine note of true love. One of the play's ironies is that the man who is most sure of himself and most grounded in reality, Malvolio, is the one who is treated as insane.

In 1987 Bill Alexander wanted to emphasize the 'madness' of all the characters, and his set and lighting plots played an integral part in this:

I wanted to stress in my production some of the links between love and madness ... to show people behaving in ways that are extreme, or deluded, or uncharacteristic – slightly 'touched' perhaps ... I wanted a sense of the intense Mediterranean heat that can go to people's heads. So the stage set was rather like a Greek island – white-washed houses, bright blue skies ... And the lighting was deliberately strong when people's behaviour was at its most illogical.[68]

The white-washed walls of the set and the intense white lighting, specifically plotted for moments of 'deranged' behaviour, also encouraged a visual association with the white walls of a padded cell. This focus on madness was pursued to the end with a disturbing conclusion for Malvolio. Antony Sher, who played the part, 'initially presented him as a figure of broad comedy, then showed the character degenerating through appalling suffering into real madness':[69]

> [Malvolio] gives the impression of groping around in the darkness while his voice is amplified to suggest a hollow cellar ... [he] is tied to a stake like a bear and he whirls round it like some mad animal. At the end of the scene, he presses Olivia's crumpled letter against his cheek, with a tormented, hallucinated look on his face. This is an extremely powerful scene, which suggests, in a pathetic way, that the borderline between the light abuses of festive misrule and real madness has now become an extremely thin one.
>
> When Malvolio reappears on stage at the end, he is totally bedraggled and, red-eyed, tries to shield his sight from the recovered daylight. But after Feste has once more taunted him with the whirligig of time speech, Malvolio says the expected 'I'll be revenged on the whole pack of you' in a curiously slow way that ends in a singsong. When he goes away, with a strange smile on his face, one understands that the joke has really been pushed too far and that he has become truly mad.[70]

Both this production and Michael Boyd's 2005 production made use of light inspired by the scenic device used in the play, *Black Comedy* by Peter Shaffer, which takes place in the darkness:

> instead of playing it in darkness, you actually put light on the stage. So what the audience sees are people behaving as though it were completely dark ... Instead of dimming the whole stage, we would flood a certain area of it with dazzlingly bright light to delineate the dark room. Both Feste and Malvolio would have their eyes open. But it would be clear to the audience from the very first moment – by the way that they moved around the stage – that neither of them was able to see a thing.[71]

2. Bill Alexander production, 1987: Antony Sher as Malvolio, 'tied to a stake like a bear...presses Olivia's crumpled letter against his cheek with a tormented, hallucinated look on his face'.

[Michael Boyd] plays the dungeon scene in a blaze of light. Thus we don't strain to catch the sound of Malvolio's *de profundis*, but hear it and see it full-on as the rope-tethered Richard Cordery angrily prowls the stage like a captive wild animal.[72]

This being comedy rather than tragedy, the accusations of madness are usually uncovered before the characters are seriously injured, although we wonder just how far Maria and Sir Toby would have been willing to go in pursing their 'sport' to the upshot, without the self-serving interests that hold them back. Donald Sinden, who played Malvolio in 1969, believed that his degradation left him no option but suicide: 'All his dignity has gone, everything he stood for has disintegrated, what is there left for him to do? Nothing . . . I saw it as a very tragic ending . . . Malvolio's a man without any sense of humour, and therefore, a tragic man.'[73]

From Shakespeare's canon, the handling of Malvolio's torture is undoubtedly one of the most difficult scenes for a director to stage. The absurdity of the situation may have its own inherent humour, but it is a bitter and dark one, especially when we think of the usual Elizabethan treatment of the insane: in Romeo's words, 'Shut up in prison, kept without food, whipped and tormented'; Rosalind, on the madness of love, mentions 'a dark house and whip' as a cure. In Elizabethan times it was the general belief that mad people were mad because they were 'possessed' by the devil or some evil spirit. An attempt was made by a priest or 'conjuror' to exorcize the devil. If this failed, as it usually did, the poor unfortunate would be manacled and chained to the wall of a bare, dark cell, beaten or whipped to their senses. The cruelty of the prank on Malvolio can often elicit an uncomfortable response, and modern productions rarely let the audience off the hook. Do we laugh at it? That is a factor entirely dependent on the choices that the director makes.

'Nor Wit nor Reason can My Passion Hide'

Gender confusion stands at the very heart of the amorous adventures and comic love-plots in the drama of the age of Shakespeare. The confusion starts from the fact that on the

Jacobean stage all the marriageable young women's parts in plays like *Twelfth Night* and *As You Like It* were written to be played by boys . . . Boys dressed as girls, girls dressed as boys, and (on stage) boys dressed as girls dressed as boys, all apparently add to the delicious pleasure of the erotic chase. Outside the close confines of marital love, family and reproduction, gender-bending is the name of the game – 'as you like it', or 'what you will'.[74]

The influential Polish critic Jan Kott asserted that 'Illyria is a country of erotic madness'.[75] As evident as it may seem to a modern audience, this aspect had not been explored until the 1970s.

Peter Gill's sexually charged revival in 1974 was dominated by a large image of Narcissus – 'a continuous reminder to the audience of the themes of ambiguous sexuality and erotic self-deception':[76]

All arc intoxicated with their own reflections, and the function of Viola and Sebastian is to put them through an Ovidian obstacle course from which they learn to turn away from the mirror and form real attachments.[77]

There is nothing at all equivocal about the physical relationships. Orsino hugs Cesario to his breast with rapturous abandon: Antonio is plainly Sebastian's long time boy friend: and Viola all but tears her hair in anguish at Olivia's unfulfilled passion for her.[78]

Demonstrative physical contact pointed to the nature of the developing relationships. As Orsino sat listening to music, lounging on cushions, Viola/Cesario sat between his legs. On asking Cesario if he had ever been in love, they playfully rolled around:

The Duke is young and lolls about panting and sighing, half-dressed, a sexy man, all male comradely affection with his courtiers, arms around them, head on shoulders on the huge Habitat cushions. And among them, Viola, small, white and utterly frozen as he fondles her/him while he talks about this other love – frozen not just with horror but with tense, deliberately fraught repression.[79]

3. Peter Gill production, 1974: John Price as Orsino (right) lolling on cushions as Jane Lapotaire as Viola is 'small, white and utterly frozen . . . not just with horror but with tense, deliberately fraught repression'.

Jane Lapotaire played a very boyish Cesario. She said, 'Viola takes her boyhood very seriously – she has to in order to survive.'[80] Olivia's reaction to the reunion of Sebastian and Viola was comical. Wardle described her as 'licking her lips at the sight of the interchangeably delicious twins': 'her "Most wonderful!" brought the house down. On "Cesario, come!" Orsino caught the wrong twin. Olivia as she moved away with Sebastian, looked back half wistfully at Viola, perhaps wishing that it were after all possible to have both.'[81]

It was not until 2001 that such an overtly sexual reading was revisited: Lindsay Posner 'cleverly locates his production in the Edwardian age of uncertainty, when young feminists and suffragettes were derided as unwomanly and dandyish male aesthetes reckoned no better than effeminate':[82]

Orsino's caressing of Cesario's head as they listen to the 'food of love' seems far from blameless. When we first meet Sebastian, Viola's long-lost twin, he's getting himself together after a romp on a large bed with Antonio . . . the butch black sailor who's plucked him from the waves. Can this really be the Sebastian who will resolve all by taking Cesario's place in Olivia's bed and maybe even in her affections? As for Matilda Ziegler's simpering Sloane of an Olivia, the kiss she plants on Viola in the

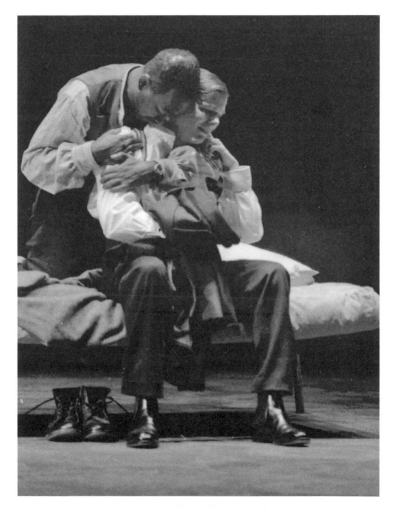

4. Lindsay Posner production, 2001: Ben Meyjes as Sebastian 'getting himself together after a romp on a large bed with Antonio . . . the butch black sailor who's plucked him from the waves' (with Joseph Mydell as Antonio).

denouement suggests the root cause of her trouble was that her real taste had always been for laddish lasses in uniform. Much of this is amusing enough . . . but the rather tactless outing of sexual ambivalence undermines the subtlety of Shakespeare's own games with the chemistry of love.[83]

Zoë Waites and Matilda Ziegler decided that on the line 'Love sought is good, but given unsought is better' (3.1.159):

> Olivia should kiss Viola . . . Lindsay's suggestion was that after Olivia initiated the kiss, Viola, rather than pulling away instantly, should respond for a brief moment. Lindsay's intention was to highlight the sexual ambiguity that reverberates through the play . . . Although Viola's instinct might initially be to pull away, the experience of such a loving kiss became fleetingly seductive for her too. Brimful as she is with love for Orsino, she is living with her own unexpressed erotic charge and readiness, and the joy, or comfort, of sensual human contact is not to be underestimated![84]

The relationship between Antonio and Sebastian in recent times has often been played as a sexual one. Director John Caird believes that this a vital misreading:

> [Antonio] deserves gratitude, friendship, filial love – all the most pure things. In other words, he has built Sebastian into something of an idol, and that is one of the most powerful forms of love there is. But if you make it sexual . . . then you diminish the other much more important aspects of the play that surround it.[85]

Conversely, Terry Hands believes that 'It's a wonderful mirror to the Orsino–Cesario relationship . . . but also enables us to see doom very clearly in front of our eyes and to relate that to the other love stories in the play.'[86]

> Antonio sees things as they are, deals in the every-day realities of a relationship, while the lovers discover perhaps more heady and ambiguous truths by dalliance and impulse. Antonio is as much

an outsider in his way as Feste and Malvolio are in theirs ... The lovers swirl and exit, perhaps still wrongly paired, it matters not; but they leave Antonio stranded in front of the painted Narcissus, a baffled figure.[87]

It seems that in the last fifty years all possible sexual permeations have been explored. But does the overt imposing of a sexual reading to every character connected with the love plot provide maybe one dynamic too many? John Caird, who directed *Twelfth Night* for the RSC in 1983, pointed to what he felt was key about Viola's male/female persona:

> Viola puts on men's clothes and behaves like a boy, she finds out what life is like in both camps, and by the end of the play she is more sexually complete than she was before. The male and the female have been married in her. Sebastian is going through a similar sort of journey. He is having a relationship of one sort or another with a man in which his masculinity is made passive.[88]

It is only on breaking the social conventions of their sex that the characters can meet on a spiritual level outside the affectations of courtly love. We see Orsino reverting to type when he refers to Viola as his 'fancy's queen'. The formulaic modes of communication which had been broken down by Viola's disguise appear to be reinstalled. Cesario, the catalyst of sexual turmoil, has gone, leaving behind him self-awareness – an understanding of both male and female aspects of the self, for all the lovers involved. As a Lord of Misrule he has been more successful than Feste.

'This Fellow is Wise Enough to Play the Fool'

> The Fool knows that the only true madness is to recognize the world as rational.[89]

Between the worlds of festivity and reality, self-delusion and sanity, sits Feste. He has been played variously as the orchestrator of the play's action, knowing commentator on the folly of the lovers, and even elevated 'to an almost superhuman position'.[90] This enigmatic character is 'rarely played as genuinely funny'.[91] The melancholic nature of his songs and his bitterly humorous remarks place him outside the 'comic' plots, with the effect that in many productions the play is depicted from Feste's viewpoint. Prefiguring Shakespeare's Fool in *King Lear*, his witticisms attempt to awaken various characters to their 'irrational' behaviour, the affectations which keep them from reality: Olivia from her mourning, Orsino from his romantic delusions. Maria and Sir Toby use him to mock his true function when confronting Malvolio as 'Sir Topas' with the converse aim of turning a sane but deluded man into a madman.

In an innovative reading of the part for Michael Boyd's 2005 production, Forbes Masson played Feste as an integral part of the play's action rather than the usual external observer. An extra dimension was given to the subplot by Feste's obviously hopeless love for Maria. The theme of unrequited love was extended to engulf his world and infiltrate his songs, with the effect that he is commenting as much on himself as on the Orsino–Viola–Olivia love triangle. After the interval we intruded on Feste alone at the piano playing a beautifully pained and sonorous melancholy song, the same he played for Orsino at the start of the play. On Viola's entry he started, as if caught betraying something of himself that he'd rather not show. Not the usual eager force in the plot to bring about the downfall of Malvolio, he walked off the stage in disgust at Maria's device, instantly seeing through her prank as a means to Sir Toby's bed. Painfully aware that he was losing her affection fast, Feste was kept dangling and manipulated by Maria with intimate touches and kisses. Reluctantly he plays the part of 'Sir Topas', hoping that the trick will win her favour. One had the sense that Feste knew the inevitable upshot of the plot but, a victim of fate and his own affections, had to play out the game.

At the end of the play when Feste lamented 'the whirligig of time brings in his revenges', he intimated that the revenge was also upon him. Maria had married and carried away the leglessly drunk Sir Toby, and he has incurred the displeasure of Olivia for his part in the deception of Malvolio. His final song was sung with anger and

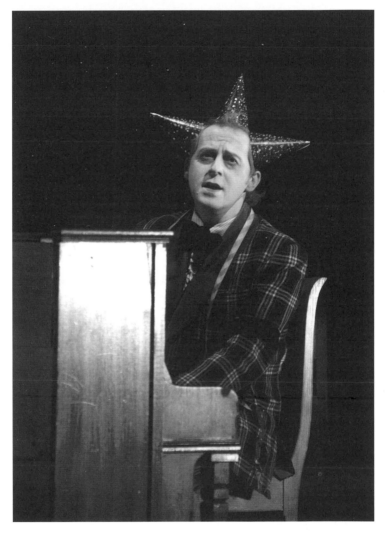

5. Forbes Masson as Feste in Michael Boyd's 2005 production: 'After the interval we intruded on Feste alone at the piano playing a beautifully pained and sonorous melancholy song.'

helpless frustration. Starting with a beautifully sung lament, the tone changed after the first verse and he angrily spat out the words 'knaves and thieves' and 'toss-pots still had drunken heads'. Used and cast aside by Maria for a particularly vile and drunken Sir Toby, the audience were made painfully aware till the end that the clown who strives to please us every day, suffers while we laugh:

> In his chequered suit and with every weary mark of distress writ large upon his whited face, Forbes Masson gives as affecting a performance as I can remember. He sings exceptionally well, accompanies himself on a pub piano and gets the balance between pain and redemptive levity exactly right. He perfectly captures the pathos of his rejection by Meg Fraser's cruelly teasing Maria before magnificently picking up his spirits with 'I am gone, sir, and anon, sir'.[92]

Nigel Hess, the composer for the 1994 Ian Judge production, pointed out that the songs contained in the play are hugely emotional and important and that the actor playing Feste has to be a skilled singer. 'Every time Feste sings everybody on stage says, "What a beautiful voice". It has to be like that.'[93] The difficulty of finding an actor talented enough to take on the role of Feste *and* sing has made this phenomenon a rarity. In 1974, though, Ron Pember, in a highly praised performance, 'sang his songs with the gritty voice of the modern, unaccompanied folk-singer'.[94] Probably the most vicious Feste on the RSC's stage, Pember brought in an element of class-consciousness, which accounted for the bitter essence at the heart of the character:

> He was a working man among the leisured classes, deeply critical of their behaviour and bitterly dissatisfied with his own ... [He] spoke like a Londoner, dressed like a faded Harlequin now reduced to busking, and hinted always at a radical's social distaste for the antics of privilege. He despised the effeteness of Orsino's court, and his angry assumption that Viola considered him a beggar ... had all the spikiness of class-pride ... He was discomforting, an outsider, almost malevolently saturnine,

defying the sentimental response to Malvolio's plight by pressing home his final accusations with heartless accuracy in Act V.[95]

The most effective, highly-praised performances of Feste came from interpretations that focused on the more bitter, melancholic aspects of his character. Difficulties with the accessibility of his 'jokes' have led to a conscious move away from Feste as 'comic' fool to a focus on his more serious function within the play. At his most sublime, the pain he imparts to the audience derives from the fact that Feste sees the world too clearly. In every aspect of light he sees darkness, in every character of worth he sees a flaw. As a melancholy entertainer, a *corrupter of words*, aware of the follies of love and class, Feste can remind us of Shakespeare himself, who strives to please his audience regardless of the pain that they and he are subject to when the festivities are over, when the play has ended.

The critic Anne Barton believed that, from a modern perspective, this comedy with its great undertow of melancholy linked the two halves of Shakespeare's working life:

The play crowns, almost summarizes, the nine Elizabethan comedies he had already produced. Children separated at sea, a heroine forced to disguise herself as a boy, the wise fool, a girl who reluctantly woos her own rival in love, ill considered vows, confusion between twins: these are only a few of the themes which *Twelfth Night* picks up and elaborates from its predecessors. At the same time, this comedy prefigures the final romances.[96]

Twelfth Night was also written around the same time as *Hamlet*, with Shakespeare's other major tragedies, *Othello*, *King Lear* and *Macbeth*, still ahead of him and, in its mixture of comedy and tragedy, foreshadows the so-called problem plays, *All's Well that Ends Well* and *Measure for Measure*. As Janice Wardle points out, *Twelfth Night* is:

One face, one voice, one habit, and two persons!
A Natural Perspective, that is and is not.

Much of the play is light-hearted in character, with the comic potential of concealed and mistaken identities running rife. But the other 'person' of the play is altogether less frivolous: many critics argue that the dominant mood of the play is sombre and dark, with its emphasis on self-deception and the transience of life and love.[97]

Illyria is a land which encompasses all the worlds that Shakespeare inhabits: 'How curious a land is this – how full of untold story, of *tragedy and laughter*, and the rich legacy of human life; shadowed with a tragic past, and big with future promise!'[98]

THE DIRECTOR'S CUT: INTERVIEWS WITH SAM MENDES, DECLAN DONNELLAN AND NEIL BARTLETT

Sam Mendes was born in 1965 and began directing classic drama both for the RSC and on the West End stage soon after his graduation from Cambridge University. In the 1990s, he was Artistic Director of the intimate Donmar Warehouse in London. His first movie, *American Beauty* (1999), won Oscars for both Best Picture and Best Director. His 1998 Donmar production of *Twelfth Night* (staged in repertoire with Chekhov's *Uncle Vanya* as his valedictory shows as the theatre's Artistic Director), which he talks about here, featured Emily Watson as Viola, Helen McCrory as Olivia and Simon Russell Beale as Malvolio.

Declan Donnellan is joint founder and Artistic Director of the highly successful theatre company Cheek by Jowl, with the designer Nick Ormerod, his partner. Born in England of Irish parents in 1953, he grew up in London and read English and Law at Cambridge University. He was called to the Bar at Middle Temple in 1978. For Cheek by Jowl he has directed many Shakespeare plays, including a hugely acclaimed all-male *As You Like It*. He has also directed for the RSC and the National Theatre, and has worked extensively in Russia, including a *Winter's Tale* for the Maly Drama Theatre of St Petersburg. In 2000 he formed a company of actors in Moscow, under the auspices of the Chekhov Festival, whose productions include Pushkin's *Boris Godunov*, Chekhov's *Three Sisters* and the *Twelfth Night* that he talks about here, which was brought to the RSC Complete Works Festival in 2007.

Neil Bartlett, born in 1958, is a director, performer, translator and writer. He was an early member of the theatre company Complicite, and has directed at the National Theatre, the Royal Court, the Goodman in Chicago and the American Repertory Theater in Boston. From 1988 to 1998 he was a member of GLORIA, with whom he created thirteen original pieces including *Sarrasine* and *A Vision of Love Revealed in Sleep*; from 1994 to 2005 he was Artistic Director of the Lyric Hammersmith in London, where his thirty-one productions included stagings of Wilde, Maugham, Shaw, Rattigan, Stevenson, Dickens, Britten, Shakespeare, Molière, Marivaux, Balzac, Genet and Kleist. He has written plays, acclaimed novels and a book mediating gay experience through the figure of Oscar Wilde (*Who Was That Man*). His RSC productions include *Romeo and Juliet* and the gender-bending Edwardian-dress 2007 Courtyard Theatre *Twelfth Night* that he talks about here.

What does the title mean to you?

SM: It's a mystery to me. I can see why he chose not to call it 'Malvolio' in the Folio, as it is so much larger than that, and I can see why he chose not to call it *What You Will*, as it sounds too much like *As You Like It*. But I think the title that he ended up with seems to promise a night of revelry, festivity and disorder, and that of course is not what the play is. So I've always suspected it was a last-minute compromise!

DD: *Twelfth Night*, for me, is a highly significant title. Twelfth Night, or 6 January, is the occasion for the Feast of Fools when masters and servants reversed status and played each other. But more significantly Twelfth Night is also the Feast of the Epiphany. A solemn feast of the Catholic church, it is the night of the Magi's visit to the Christ child. But the significance of the visit is immense, for it was the first moment when people in our world realized who Jesus actually was. His significance was understood. This moment of realization or revelation is central to Christian thinking, as it is the moment when the immanent is made manifest. The moment of human perception of the divine. Many writers, like James Joyce, were deeply concerned with this moment, and Shakespeare's plays are full of epiphanic revelations.

For example, in many of the comedies, the heroine, filled with the spirit of active love, goes into disguise and her final unmasking is epiphanic. But we don't need to know the word 'epiphany' to feel what it is. Falling in love can have the quality of epiphany, of understanding not so much a new thing, as suddenly and gloriously realizing what was always waiting there. When we feel 'I love you' we may also feel 'I will always love you', but when that love is very deep, we may also have the uncanny feeling 'and I have always loved you!' When Viola and Sebastian recognize each other in mysterious images of time, change and death, we are moved because it connects with our own sense of falling in love, with epiphany. On the other hand, the tragedy of Othello resides in his being unable to recognize this love in Desdemona.

NB: The play is written under the sign of festivity, of license, of misbehaviour. But it's not called 'First Night'; this is the time when things go a bit too far, when people are at the end of their tether . . .

In Shakespeare's time, Illyria was a state on the Adriatic coast (Croatia today), but the name is also evocative of 'illusion' and 'lyric' ('If music be . . .') and 'Elysium': so should we think of it as a place of reality or of fantasy? And did your thinking along those lines shape you and your designer's choice of set, costumes and temporal location?

SM: I didn't think of it as a place of reality at all. For me it was a place of illusion. The thing that came most to my mind when I was working on it was *Alice Through the Looking Glass* – Lewis Carroll's twisted logic, his peculiar brand of English melancholy. We even had Viola step through a looking glass. I tried very hard right from the start to create a sense of it being a dreamscape. When Emily Watson, who played Viola, arrived in Illyria she was talking to a succession of mysterious figures in the shadows – one wasn't sure if she was awake or dreaming. And yet, rather like Lewis Carroll, once we entered this world, once we went down the rabbit hole, there were many things about it that reminded us of England, and of a specific social structure. When we took it to Brooklyn Academy of Music in New York, beyond the mirror was an enormous pool, almost like a lake, covered with floating candles. Candles were also suspended over the acting area in both directions. That was a nod to the candlelight by which the play might first have been performed, and also to the sense of Christmas time and of Twelfth Night itself, but that gave it an even more dreamlike feel. So our Illyria had a firmly non-naturalistic framework holding within it something resembling a real world.

DD: All of Shakespeare's plays take place first and foremost on a stage, and this space changes and articulates shifting worlds and different realities. For example, in the history plays Shakespeare is not putting the 'real' medieval world on stage but creating another theatrical world. We cannot understand Shakespeare if we reduce him to an everyday naturalism or historical accuracy. If we get locked in the merciless logic of spatial or indeed psychological logic, we miss the point.

In *Twelfth Night* Shakespeare presents a number of different worlds. There is the world of Olivia's house which is very different to Orsino's court; running between them is the dangerous space of the path that separates these masculine and feminine spaces. Danger hides on this path, but so does love. Pirates get arrested but rings are found.

For me as a director, 'space' is the very first challenge to be investigated. Investigating the worlds of Shakespeare's plays is the first step in all our rehearsals.

NB: I think you have to play for real, and let the fantastical take care of itself – at least you do when you are working in The Courtyard Theatre, where no one needs to be told they are in the world of theatre and make-believe. There were certain specific realities I wanted to root the play in. It is a play about the strictly hierarchical, upstairs/downstairs life of two aristocratic country houses. It is a play in which homoeroticism has to be part of the cultural zeitgeist, so that neither Antonio's homosexuality nor Orsino's . . . confusion (!) need any great explanation. It is a play in which we have to take for granted that a single woman as intelligent and wealthy as Olivia can both dream of running her own life and yet absolutely be denied that possibility by her society – i.e. everyone expects that she should marry her neighbour now that her brother and father are both dead. A costume-drama version of the turn of the nineteenth century seemed to provide all the right clues . . . but apart from the costumes, the stage was bare – letting the words and the music and the laughs do the work.

In one obvious respect our production was 'fantastical' – in order to provide more good roles for women than is normally possible in a Shakespeare company, I cast three actresses in three of the male roles, capitalizing on the fact that cross-dressing and sexual license and low comedy are all central to both the atmosphere and the mechanics of this particular play. If men can drag up on *Twelfth Night*, then surely women can too.

Social status is a big part of the comedy. Did that also affect the period and setting you chose for the play?

SM: Yes, the world of the play needs a hierarchy, especially in Olivia's household. So that of course did affect the settings and clothes. I feel you do need to sense that Sir Toby and Maria are somehow 'below stairs' in the servants' quarters; you need a sense that Malvolio is a steward, that Fabian is a footman of some sort. Beyond that, the one character who I felt needed to be defined and clarified by costuming was Feste. My feeling with all Shakespearean fools is that they need to be firmly rooted in the world of the play; the moment they stand outside it and don the comedy checked suit and a little trilby your heart sinks. So for me, Feste was a tramp, a drifter; he's been in the household before, he's gone away for a while, he's moneyless, he travels with a knapsack and his guitar. It seemed to me to be very important that you get the sense of him as somebody who might be found on a street corner, with his cap in hand, begging for coins. He's obviously impoverished and he obviously needs to earn a crust. That was important, as it somewhat clarified his dislike of Malvolio.

And of course for Malvolio's downfall to work he needs to be established as a household steward. Then when he attempts to seduce Olivia, he is attempting to subvert the social order, to overturn the hierarchy of the household.

DD: Our approach to the play and its period and setting is fluid throughout the rehearsal process; but of course no human beings have ever invented any world devoid of status or hierarchy (though many have died in the attempt!).

NB: See my previous answer!

Shakespeare had boy–girl twins, who are never identical, but mistaken identity is at the heart of the play: how much of a factor is the 'identical twin' question in casting Viola and Sebastian?

SM: I remember casting *Troilus and Cressida* at the RSC when Nick Hytner was also casting *King Lear*, and Nick said, 'Oh, how much the twins look alike is the sort of thing that boring people talk about in the car on the way home!' Clearly you shouldn't cast two people who look wildly different, but whatever they look like, two good actors will move you in that final reconciliation scene come what may – it's a beautiful scene. Beyond that, dress them in the same clothes, the same hat, and if they're vaguely the same height that should be enough.

DD: To a certain degree, and we would certainly avoid choosing actors who looked wildly different, but we also rely on the fact that the audience have both the desire and the capacity to suspend their disbelief!

NB: Provided that one isn't a foot shorter than the other, the rest is acting – and pacing; if you stage the 'near misses' of one scene moving into another right, then the audience does all the work of the doubling for you.

What does disguise – and playing at gender-bending in particular – do for Viola?

DD: I think it's more important to ask what these elements do for us. The complexity of love and particularly the fragility of human desire and sexuality is so crafted by Shakespeare that most, if not all, of his plays leave us asking questions about ourselves. Certainly the ambivalence of sexuality as it is figured by Shakespeare in *Twelfth Night* transcends most modern reductions into gay and straight.

NB: Initially, it allows her to maintain some privacy while she sorts herself out – then it allows her everything; to lie, to flirt, to be with men . . . to explore herself. She needs to do this, because she's a powerless girl: Olivia and Maria manage to do all of those things without cross-dressing, but they're older, and wiser – and desperate!

'Cesario, come – For so you shall be, while you are a man': whereas Rosalind in *As You Like It* and Portia in *The Merchant of Venice* return at the end in female garb, Viola remains in male. We're even told that the Captain who is looking after her women's clothes has been imprisoned at the behest of Malvolio. Is this just a technicality: there's no time for a quick change? Or does it go deeper?

SM: I don't think Shakespeare ever does something like that accidentally. I think it does run deeper. I think the sexual ambiguity, which he plays on the whole time, is something he wants to linger on at the end, and I think it makes it much more interesting. You could say that what fascinates Shakespeare most of all are the unfinished stories, Iago, Leontes, Jaques – and here, of course, Malvolio. 'I'll be revenged on the whole pack of you' is the line that hangs over the end of the play even more than Viola's last moments, or 'The Wind And The Rain'.

NB: Yes, it goes deeper – if Viola is played by a young man. Both Orsino and the audience (at least in our production) hugely enjoyed the fact that he is 'really' getting off with a gorgeous boy at the curtain call. It explains such a lot about him, don't you think?

Orsino can sometimes seem a rather shallow courtly lover in the opening act, then he's offstage for a very long time before his return at the end: does this present peculiar problems for a director and an actor?

SM: Orsino's a much better part than people think. I don't think it does present a problem. Mark Strong was sensational in the role. I think he's lovesick: in other words he's in love with the exquisite pain of being in love – a love that is unrequited. So once you've established that he is actually hungry for that state, is trapped in it, and is almost unwilling to come out of it, I think it's a wonderful part. Very funny actually, and rather touching. So it didn't strike me as an issue.

DD: It is structurally curious; rather like the absence of Posthumus through the middle of *Cymbeline*, but this is possibly explained by the fact that the actor playing Orsino may been playing another part. Orsino may have doubled as Maria – in which case the actor playing Orsino would probably have been rather short!

NB: If you think he's shallow in his first scene, then you definitely have a problem. If, however, you think he is a powerful portrait of a powerful man – handsome, charismatic, sexy, obsessed, passionate – with some of the most drop-dead lines in the (or any) play, then you're all set for a great evening. If you think obsessive behaviour, sexual ambiguity and laughable human folly are 'shallow', then you shouldn't be directing *Twelfth Night* . . .

Are we meant to believe in the marriage between Sebastian and Olivia?

SM: Yes. I think the easy way out when you direct it is to ironize those things in the last acts of Shakespearean comedies. The really difficult thing to do, like at the end of *The Winter's Tale* when Camillo and Paulina suddenly pair off, is to make the audience believe it. You could say that the real challenge of the play is to make these impossible moments seem possible.

DD: The triangle of Sebastian, Antonio and Olivia is complex. Both Antonio and Olivia give Sebastian money, which you notice he never manages to refuse. Olivia herself has the line: 'For youth is bought more oft than begged or borrowed', which is remarkable. Certainly Sebastian's conversion from Antonio's love-object to Olivia's is very fast. It's hard not to believe that this rapid change is not lubricated by cash. Even Orsino is impressed by Olivia's wealth!

However, who are we to judge? When Sebastian sees the new sun, he sees that it is glorious. Perhaps he is more sincere than he seems. Perhaps he has been transfigured by love, like his sister. We often forget that Sebastian also disguises himself as Roderigo at the beginning of the play. Why should he do this? He is a complex character and far removed from a two-dimensional juvenile lead.

NB: Well...it's not going to last very long, is it? He's over the moon – she's rich, beautiful and (best of all, if you're a horny teenager who rather enjoys people falling in love with him) she is sexually and emotionally impulsive. She, however, is humiliated, furious, trapped in a marriage even more ridiculous than the one she escaped from with Orsino. Hardly a recipe for success. On the other hand, he is a very handsome young man, and well educated, and so who knows...

Music seems particularly important in this play. What implications did that have for your production? And what about Feste's songs in particular?

SM: Huge. Music starts the play, and sets its tone. It's crucial. It seems to me that when songs are sung, unlike any other play in the canon with the possible exception of *As You Like It*, people simply sit and listen to them. 'Come Away Death' and 'O Mistress Mine', they sit and listen, and then at the end we the audience sit and listen to 'The Wind And The Rain'. They're very static songs: even at the beginning with 'If music be the food of love, play on', Orsino sits and listens. The act of listening to music is actually pivotal, it's central to the play. The music itself, therefore, has to have an emotional resonance. I was really pleased with the music, which was written by George Stiles. It's one of the things that I remember most from the production.

DD: Music is integral to all our work. We began rehearsals by investigating the space through music, thus music was always crucial to our investigation. Feste's songs are crucial as he is the paid entertainer, exactly akin to the actors onstage.

6. Feste's songs are crucial 'as he is the paid entertainer, exactly akin to the actors onstage': Igor Yasulovich as Feste and Dmitry Dyuzhev as Sir Andrew in Declan Donnellan's 2007 production during the RSC Complete Works Festival.

NB: Music is in the heart of the play. It opens it and closes it. The music is incredibly interior – apart from the 'catch' scene, all the music is about hidden emotion. The last song, for instance, is the exact opposite of the communal merrymaking that usually closed an Elizabethan comedy...that's why I put Feste and his grand piano in the centre of the stage. For all its glorious mechanics, it's a very introspective play...it probes the heart, which is music's job.

At the beginning of the play Feste has returned after an unexplained absence. Did you and your actor feel it necessary to devise a 'back-story' in order to get inside Feste's character?

DD: Well I have worked with five different Festes over the years and with each we discussed what might have happened previously, his possible reasons for leaving the house, and each time I think we came up with different conclusions! But such work is crucial to give authority to the actor. Incidentally, most of these 'discussions' would have taken the form of physical exercises.

NB: Well he's a musician, and a comedian, and they're always temperamental bastards . . . Olivia just kicked him out for a while, and he needed the work, so he's been moonlighting at Orsino's.

How did you stage the great letter scene?

SM: Once we decided to place it inside his bedroom it unlocked all sorts of interesting things. Because it was in his private space you immediately got drawn into his private fantasy world in a much more serious way. There was a sense that he did this all the time, that he had a very vivid fantasy world which involved him and Olivia on a regular basis. This wasn't new, it was something that he'd already been fantasizing about for years. He lay on his bed and was clearly about to indulge in a sexual fantasy, and there was a feeling that we shouldn't be in this room with him, and neither should Sir Toby, Andrew and Fabian, who were hiding behind the screen.

DD: We decided to take the character of Malvolio absolutely seriously. This made the pain and humiliation that Malvolio experiences all the more serious and real, which in turn made it all the more funny. Comedy always has its feet in pain!

NB: It staged itself. We were working on a bare stage, and didn't need a box-tree because we already had a grand piano to hide behind, so it was just a question of working out, move by move, how three people could hide from a fourth on a bare stage as he shared his predicament with audience . . . my only rule was that he could never stand still or face one way for very long – otherwise there's no gag, they're just safely upstage and he's safely downstage. The whole point is that the scene is a virtuoso demonstration of the fact that love is blind; even though they're right there with him, he never sees them. Of course it helps if your Malvolio (John Lithgow) is six foot three and a natural physical clown.

Sir Toby and Sir Andrew are often perceived as especially lovable characters, but Malvolio's view of them as idle drunken parasites is not without justice, is it?

SM: No, I think they're complete liggers [free-loaders, gate-crashers]! They're total leeches, especially Sir Toby. They live off other people, they don't do a stroke of work. But at the same time they're not entirely wrong when they seem to ask, 'What's the point?' For me, the key to Sir Toby and Sir Andrew is that they're older characters, coming into the twilight of their lives, dealing with past disappointments and learning to come to terms with compromise. They're not young and vivacious, they're drinking to stave off melancholy, and to forget. There's a tangible sense of disappointment about them and Toby's cruelty emerges out of that: his own self-loathing, his own sense of regret. However, it is Sir Toby who in many ways drives the action of the play, particularly in the second half.

DD: No, I think there are things to be said for and against all of Shakespeare's characters. Shakespeare is anti-sentimental and he is great precisely because he is non-judgemental about his characters. Like Chekhov, Shakespeare invites us to draw our own conclusions about the characters he presents.

NB: Some of my best friends are idle, drunken parasites. What's your point?

Is the gulling of Malvolio taken too far, when it comes to the darkened room? And does he recover his dignity at the end of the play? Whether or not his final exit line ('I'll be revenged . . .') gets a laugh – or what kind of laugh it gets – is often the test of a production.

SM: Too far compared to what? It's taken as far as it needs to be taken in order to articulate the darkness in the story. I pushed it as far as I possibly could without distorting it. I think it tips over into cruelty, yes. I think that there is a streak of cruelty in Feste. He taunts Malvolio beyond what might seem funny or humane. I love those moments when darkness enters the comedies, they are the most exciting for me. Does Malvolio recover his dignity? Well, he recovers his seriousness: whether he recovers his dignity is in a way up to the director and the actor. You can have him recover his seriousness then have him walk off with his clothes flapping around his heels and he's funny. I didn't want him to make him funny. I wanted to make him frightening.

I didn't go into this production with a set of preconceived ideas or a heavily conceptual framework. I went into it with an open mind, and it was very unformed, image-based ideas that seemed to lead me. The only idea I presented to Simon Russell Beale [Malvolio] at the beginning of the process was to wonder how it would be if we were given access to Malvolio's inner space. So the letter scene, which normally happens in the garden, happened in his bedroom, and the box-tree was actually a screen with a print of a box-tree on it. That unlocked a lot of different things in the role. One felt one had been shown inside Malvolio's inner sanctum, and that made him

7. Simon Russell Beale as Malvolio in Sam Mendes' 2002 production at the Donmar Warehouse in London – the letter scene set in a bedroom ('the box-tree was actually a screen with a print of a box-tree in it. That unlocked a lot of different things in the role').

8. The humiliation of Malvolio goes 'way too far. So does the humiliation of Olivia when she realizes she's married the wrong teenager': Jason Merrells as Orsino, Chris New as Viola and Justine Mitchell as Olivia in Neil Bartlett's 2007 production in The Courtyard Theatre, Stratford-upon-Avon.

seem very vulnerable. So his punishment consequently felt all the more harsh. And in part because of that, I think, the line 'I'll be revenged . . .' was met with silence. Dead silence. It wasn't funny, it was awkward. Like someone letting off an air-raid siren in the middle of a violin concerto.

DD: We had a very special way of treating the exit of Malvolio. But you need to see the Russians do it! Anyway, how far is 'too far'? There are many darknesses in the play that are unsuitable to lightweight comedy, but I don't know who could argue that *Twelfth Night* was merely a lightweight comedy.

The final grimness of *Twelfth Night* Shakespeare never lived to see. Thirty years later Malvolio came back, disguised as Oliver Cromwell, and was indeed revenged upon the whole pack of them. The puritans closed down the theatres and destroyed forever the particular form of performance that created the greatest plays ever written. But be careful, he still returns from time to time . . .

NB: Yes it goes too far, way too far. So does the humiliation of Olivia in front of everybody when it turns out she's married the wrong teenager. So does the humiliation of Orsino when Olivia publicly spurns his final offer of marriage. So does the humiliation of Antonio when 'Sebastian' denies him in public. And so on. I never want to tell an audience if a moment is tragic or comic. Some people find Malvolio's exit full of dignity and pathos. Some people think he's a deluded, jumped-up, dirty-minded old idiot who's got his comeuppance, and laugh in his face. That's called live theatre.

SHAKESPEARE'S CAREER IN THE THEATRE

BEGINNINGS

William Shakespeare was an extraordinarily intelligent man who was born and died in an ordinary market town in the English Midlands. He lived an uneventful life in an eventful age. Born in April 1564, he was the eldest son of John Shakespeare, a glove-maker who was prominent on the town council until he fell into financial difficulties. Young William was educated at the local grammar in Stratford-upon-Avon, Warwickshire, where he gained a thorough grounding in the Latin language, the art of rhetoric and classical poetry. He married Ann Hathaway and had three children (Susanna, then the twins Hamnet and Judith) before his twenty-first birthday: an exceptionally young age for the period. We do not know how he supported his family in the mid-1580s.

Like many clever country boys, he moved to the city in order to make his way in the world. Like many creative people, he found a career in the entertainment business. Public playhouses and professional full-time acting companies reliant on the market for their income were born in Shakespeare's childhood. When he arrived in London as a man, sometime in the late 1580s, a new phenomenon was in the making: the actor who is so successful that he becomes a 'star'. The word did not exist in its modern sense, but the pattern is recognizable: audiences went to the theatre not so much to see a particular show as to witness the comedian Richard Tarlton or the dramatic actor Edward Alleyn.

Shakespeare was an actor before he was a writer. It appears not to have been long before he realized that he was never going to grow into a great comedian like Tarlton or a great tragedian like Alleyn. Instead, he found a role within his company as the man who patched up old plays, breathing new life, new dramatic twists, into tired repertory pieces. He paid close attention to the work of the university-educated dramatists who were writing history plays and tragedies for the public stage in a style more ambitious, sweeping and poetically grand than anything which had been seen before. But he may also have noted that what his friend and rival Ben Jonson would call 'Marlowe's mighty line' sometimes faltered in the mode of comedy. Going to university, as Christopher Marlowe did, was all well and good for honing the arts of rhetorical elaboration and classical allusion, but it could lead to a loss of the common touch. To stay close to a large segment of the potential audience for public theatre, it was necessary to write for clowns as well as kings and to intersperse the flights of poetry with the humour of the tavern, the privy and the brothel: Shakespeare was the first to establish himself early in his career as an equal master of tragedy, comedy and history. He realized that theatre could be the medium to make the national past available to a wider audience than the elite who could afford to read large history books: his signature early works include not only the classical tragedy *Titus Andronicus* but also the sequence of English historical plays on the Wars of the Roses.

He also invented a new role for himself, that of in-house company dramatist. Where his peers and predecessors had to sell their plays to the theatre managers on a poorly-paid piecework basis, Shakespeare took a percentage of the box-office income. The Lord Chamberlain's Men constituted themselves in 1594 as a joint stock company, with the profits being distributed among the core actors who had invested as sharers. Shakespeare acted himself – he appears in the cast lists of some of Ben Jonson's plays as well as the list of actors' names at the beginning of his own collected works – but his principal duty was to write two or three plays a year for the company. By holding shares, he was effectively earning himself a royalty on his work, something no author had ever done before in England. When the Lord Chamberlain's Men collected their fee for performance at court in the Christmas season of 1594, three of them went along to the Treasurer of the Chamber: not just Richard Burbage the tragedian and Will Kempe the clown, but also Shakespeare the scriptwriter. That was something new.

The next four years were the golden period in Shakespeare's career, though overshadowed by the death of his only son Hamnet, aged eleven, in 1596. In his early thirties and in full command of both his poetic and his theatrical medium, he perfected his art of comedy, while also developing his tragic and historical writing in new ways. In 1598, Francis Meres, a Cambridge University graduate with his finger on the pulse of the London literary world, praised Shakespeare for his excellence across the genres:

> As Plautus and Seneca are accounted the best for comedy and tragedy among the Latins, so Shakespeare among the English is the most excellent in both kinds for the stage; for comedy, witness his *Gentlemen of Verona*, his *Errors*, his *Love Labours Lost*, his *Love Labours Won*, his *Midsummer Night Dream* and his *Merchant of Venice*: for tragedy his *Richard the 2*, *Richard the 3*, *Henry the 4*, *King John*, *Titus Andronicus* and his *Romeo and Juliet*.

For Meres, as for the many writers who praised the 'honey-flowing vein' of *Venus and Adonis* and *Lucrece*, narrative poems written when the theatres were closed due to plague in 1593–94, Shakespeare was marked above all by his linguistic skill, by the gift of turning elegant poetic phrases.

PLAYHOUSES

Elizabethan playhouses were 'thrust' or 'one-room' theatres. To understand Shakespeare's original theatrical life, we have to forget about the indoor theatre of later times, with its proscenium arch and curtain that would be opened at the beginning and closed at the end of each act. In the proscenium arch theatre, stage and auditorium are effectively two separate rooms: the audience looks from one world into another as if through the imaginary 'fourth wall' framed by the proscenium. The picture-frame stage, together with the elaborate scenic effects and backdrops beyond it, created the illusion of a self-contained world – especially once nineteenth-century developments in the control of artificial lighting meant that the auditorium could be darkened and the spectators made to focus on the lighted stage. Shakespeare, by contrast, wrote for a bare platform stage with a standing audience gathered around it in a courtyard in full daylight. The audience were always conscious of themselves and their fellow-spectators, and they shared the same 'room' as the actors. A sense of immediate presence and the creation of rapport with the audience were all-important. The actor could not afford to imagine he was in a closed world, with silent witnesses dutifully observing him from the darkness.

Shakespeare's theatrical career began at the Rose Theatre in Southwark. The stage was wide and shallow, trapezoid in shape, like a lozenge. This design had a great deal of potential for the theatrical equivalent of cinematic split-screen effects, whereby one group of characters would enter at the door at one end of the tiring-house wall at the back of the stage and another group through the door at the other end, thus creating two rival tableaux. Many of the battle-heavy and faction-filled plays that premiered at the Rose have scenes of just this sort.

At the rear of the Rose stage, there were three capacious exits, each over ten feet wide. Unfortunately, the very limited excavation of a fragmentary portion of the original Globe site, in 1989, revealed nothing about the stage. The first Globe was built in 1599 with similar proportions to those of another theatre, the Fortune, albeit that the former was polygonal and looked circular, whereas the latter was rectangular. The building contract for the Fortune survives and allows us to infer that the stage of the Globe was probably substantially wider than it was deep (perhaps forty-three feet wide and twenty-seven feet deep). It may well have been tapered at the front, like that of the Rose.

The capacity of the Globe was said to have been enormous, perhaps in excess of three thousand. It has been conjectured that about eight hundred people may have stood in the yard, with two thousand or more in the three layers of covered galleries. The other 'public' playhouses were also of large capacity, whereas the indoor Blackfriars theatre that Shakespeare's company began using in 1608 – the former refectory of a monastery – had overall internal dimensions of a mere forty-six by sixty feet. It would have made for a much more intimate theatrical experience and had a much smaller capacity, probably of about six hundred people. Since they paid at least sixpence a head, the Blackfriars attracted a more select or 'private' audience. The atmosphere would have been closer to that of an indoor performance before the court in the Whitehall Palace or at Richmond. That Shakespeare always wrote for indoor production at court as well as outdoor performance in the public theatre should make us cautious about inferring, as some scholars have, that the opportunity provided by the intimacy of the Blackfriars led to a significant change towards a 'chamber' style in his last plays – which, besides, were performed at both the Globe and the Blackfriars. After the occupation of the Blackfriars a five-act structure seems to have become more important to Shakespeare. That was because of artificial lighting: there were musical interludes between the acts, while the candles were trimmed and replaced. Again, though, something similar must have been necessary for indoor court performances throughout his career.

Front of house there were the 'gatherers' who collected the money from audience members: a penny to stand in the open-air yard, another penny for a place in the covered galleries, sixpence for the prominent 'lord's rooms' to the side of the stage. In the indoor 'private' theatres, gallants from the audience who fancied making themselves part of the spectacle sat on stools on the edge of the stage itself. Scholars debate as to how widespread this practice was in the public theatres such as the Globe. Once the audience were in place and the money counted, the gatherers were available to be extras on stage. That is one reason why battles and crowd scenes often come later rather than early in Shakespeare's plays. There was no formal prohibition upon performance by women, and there certainly were women among the gatherers, so it is not beyond the bounds of possibility that female crowd members were played by females.

The play began at two o'clock in the afternoon and the theatre had to be cleared by five. After the main show, there would be a jig – which consisted not only of dancing, but also of knockabout comedy (it is the origin of the farcical 'afterpiece' in the eighteenth-century theatre). So the time available for a Shakespeare play was about two and a half hours, somewhere between the 'two hours' traffic' mentioned in the prologue to *Romeo and Juliet* and the 'three hours' spectacle' referred to in the preface to the 1647 Folio of Beaumont and Fletcher's plays. The prologue to a play by Thomas Middleton refers to a thousand lines as 'one hour's words', so the likelihood is that about two and a half thousand, or a maximum of three thousand lines made up the performed text. This is indeed the length of most of Shakespeare's comedies, whereas many of his tragedies and histories are much longer, raising the possibility that he wrote full scripts, possibly with eventual publication in mind, in the full knowledge that the stage version would be heavily cut. The short Quarto texts published in his lifetime – they used to be called 'Bad' Quartos – provide fascinating evidence as to the kind of cutting that probably took place. So, for instance, the First Quarto of *Hamlet* neatly merges two occasions when Hamlet is overheard, the 'Fishmonger' and the 'nunnery' scenes.

The social composition of the audience was mixed. The poet Sir John Davies wrote of 'A thousand townsmen, gentlemen and whores, / Porters and servingmen' who would 'together throng' at the public playhouses. Though moralists associated female play-going with adultery and the sex trade, many perfectly respectable citizens' wives were regular attendees. Some, no doubt, resembled the modern groupie: a story attested in two different sources has one citizen's wife making a post-show assignation with Richard Burbage and ending up in bed with Shakespeare – supposedly eliciting from the latter the quip that William the Conqueror was before Richard III. Defenders of theatre liked to say that by witnessing the comeuppance of villains on the stage, audience members would repent of their own wrongdoings, but the reality is that most people went to the theatre then, as they do now, for entertainment more than moral edification. Besides, it would be foolish to suppose that audiences behaved in a homogeneous way: a pamphlet of the 1630s tells of how two men went to see *Pericles* and one of them laughed while the other wept. Bishop John Hall complained that people went to church for the same reasons that they went to the theatre: 'for company, for custom, for recreation . . . to feed his eyes or his ears . . . or perhaps for sleep'.

Men-about-town and clever young lawyers went to be seen as much as to see. In the modern popular imagination, shaped not least by *Shakespeare in Love* and the opening sequence of Laurence Olivier's

Henry V film, the penny-paying groundlings stand in the yard hurling abuse or encouragement and hazelnuts or orange peel at the actors, while the sophisticates in the covered galleries appreciate Shakespeare's soaring poetry. The reality was probably the other way round. A 'groundling' was a kind of fish, so the nickname suggests the penny audience standing below the level of the stage and gazing in silent open-mouthed wonder at the spectacle unfolding above them. The more difficult audience members, who kept up a running commentary of clever remarks on the performance and who occasionally got into quarrels with players, were the gallants. Like Hollywood movies in modern times, Elizabethan and Jacobean plays exercised a powerful influence on the fashion and behaviour of the young. John Marston mocks the lawyers who would open their lips, perhaps to court a girl, and out would 'flow / Naught but pure Juliet and Romeo'.

THE ENSEMBLE AT WORK

In the absence of typewriters and photocopying machines, reading aloud would have been the means by which the company got to know a new play. The tradition of the playwright reading his complete script to the assembled company endured for generations. A copy would then have been taken to the Master of the Revels for licensing. The theatre book-holder or prompter would then have copied the parts for distribution to the actors. A partbook consisted of the character's lines, with each speech preceded by the last three or four words of the speech before, the so-called 'cue'. These would have been taken away and studied or 'conned'. During this period of learning the parts, an actor might have had some one-to-one instruction, perhaps from the dramatist, perhaps from a senior actor who had played the same part before, and, in the case of an apprentice, from his master. A high percentage of Desdemona's lines occur in dialogue with Othello, of Lady Macbeth's with Macbeth, Cleopatra's with Antony and Volumnia's with Coriolanus. The roles would almost certainly have been taken by the apprentice of the lead actor, usually Burbage, who delivers the majority of the cues. Given that apprentices lodged with their masters, there would have been

9. Hypothetical reconstruction of the interior of an Elizabethan playhouse during a performance.

ample opportunity for personal instruction, which may be what made it possible for young men to play such demanding parts.

After the parts were learned, there may have been no more than a single rehearsal before the first performance. With six different plays to be put on every week, there was no time for more. Actors, then, would go into a show with a very limited sense of the whole. The notion of a collective rehearsal process that is itself a process of discovery for the actors is wholly modern and would have been incomprehensible to Shakespeare and his original ensemble. Given the number of parts an actor had to hold in his memory, the forgetting of lines was probably more frequent than in the modern theatre. The book-holder was on hand to prompt.

Backstage personnel included the property man, the tire-man who oversaw the costumes, call-boys, attendants and the musicians, who might play at various times from the main stage, the rooms above and within the tiring-house. Scriptwriters sometimes made a nuisance of themselves backstage. There was often tension between the acting companies and the freelance playwrights from whom they purchased scripts: it was a smart move on the part of Shakespeare and the Lord Chamberlain's Men to bring the writing process in-house.

Scenery was limited, though sometimes set-pieces were brought on (a bank of flowers, a bed, the mouth of hell). The trapdoor from below, the gallery stage above and the curtained discovery-space at the back allowed for an array of special effects: the rising of ghosts and apparitions, the descent of gods, dialogue between a character at a window and another at ground level, the revelation of a statue or a pair of lovers playing at chess. Ingenious use could be made of props, as with the ass's head in *A Midsummer Night's Dream*. In a theatre that does not clutter the stage with the material paraphernalia of everyday life, those objects that are deployed may take on powerful symbolic weight, as when Shylock bears his weighing scales in one hand and knife in the other, thus becoming a parody of the figure of Justice who traditionally bears a sword and a balance. Among the more significant items in the property cupboard of Shakespeare's company, there would have been a throne (the 'chair of state'), joint stools, books, bottles, coins, purses, letters (which are brought on stage, read or referred to on about eighty occasions in the complete works), maps, gloves, a set of stocks (in which Kent is put in *King Lear*), rings, rapiers, daggers, broadswords, staves, pistols, masks and vizards, heads and skulls, torches and tapers and lanterns which served to signal night scenes on the daylit stage, a buck's head, an ass's head, animal costumes. Live animals also put in appearances, most notably the dog Crab in *The Two Gentlemen of Verona* and possibly a young polar bear in *The Winter's Tale*.

The costumes were the most important visual dimension of the play. Playwrights were paid between £2 and £6 per script, whereas Alleyn was not averse to paying £20 for 'a black velvet cloak with sleeves embroidered all with silver and gold'. No matter the period of the play, actors always wore contemporary costume. The excitement for the audience came not from any impression of historical accuracy, but from the richness of the attire and perhaps the transgressive thrill of the knowledge that here were commoners like themselves strutting in the costumes of courtiers in effective defiance of the strict sumptuary laws whereby in real life people had to wear the clothes that befitted their social station.

To an even greater degree than props, costumes could carry symbolic importance. Racial characteristics could be suggested: a breastplate and helmet for a Roman soldier, a turban for a Turk, long robes for exotic characters such as Moors, a gabardine for a Jew. The figure of Time, as in *The Winter's Tale*, would be equipped with hourglass, scythe and wings; Rumour, who speaks the prologue of *2 Henry IV*, wore a costume adorned with a thousand tongues. The wardrobe in the tiring-house of the Globe would have contained much of the same stock as that of rival manager Philip Henslowe at the Rose: green gowns for outlaws and foresters, black for melancholy men such as Jaques and people in mourning such as the Countess in *All's Well that Ends Well* (at the beginning of *Hamlet*, the prince is still in mourning black when everyone else is in festive garb for the wedding of the new king), a gown and hood for a friar (or a feigned friar like the duke in *Measure for Measure*), blue coats and tawny to distinguish the followers of rival factions, a leather apron and ruler for a carpenter (as in the opening scene of *Julius Caesar* – and in *A Midsummer Night's Dream*, where this is the only sign that Peter Quince is a carpenter), a cockle hat with staff and a pair of sandals for a pilgrim or palmer (the disguise assumed by Helen in *All's Well*), bodices and kirtles with farthingales beneath for the boys who are to be dressed as girls. A gender switch such as that of Rosalind or Jessica seems to have taken between fifty and eighty lines of dialogue – Viola does not resume her 'maiden weeds', but remains in her boy's costume to the end of *Twelfth Night* because a change would have slowed down the action at just the moment it was speeding to a climax. Henslowe's inventory also included 'a robe for to go invisible': Oberon, Puck and Ariel must have had something similar.

As the costumes appealed to the eyes, so there was music for the ears. Comedies included many songs. Desdemona's willow song, perhaps a late addition to the text, is a rare and thus exceptionally poignant example from tragedy. Trumpets and tuckets sounded for ceremonial entrances, drums denoted an army on the march. Background music could create atmosphere, as at the beginning of *Twelfth Night*, during the lovers' dialogue near the end of

The Merchant of Venice, when the statue seemingly comes to life in *The Winter's Tale*, and for the revival of Pericles and of Lear (in the Quarto text, but not the Folio). The haunting sound of the hautboy suggested a realm beyond the human, as when the god Hercules is imagined deserting Mark Antony. Dances symbolized the harmony of the end of a comedy – though in Shakespeare's world of mingled joy and sorrow, someone is usually left out of the circle.

The most important resource was, of course, the actors themselves. They needed many skills: in the words of one contemporary commentator, 'dancing, activity, music, song, elocution, ability of body, memory, skill of weapon, pregnancy of wit'. Their bodies were as significant as their voices. Hamlet tells the player to 'suit the action to the word, the word to the action': moments of strong emotion, known as 'passions', relied on a repertoire of dramatic gestures as well as a modulation of the voice. When Titus Andronicus has had his hand chopped off, he asks 'How can I grace my talk, / Wanting a hand to give it action?' A pen portrait of 'The Character of an Excellent Actor' by the dramatist John Webster is almost certainly based on his impression of Shakespeare's leading man, Richard Burbage: 'By a full and significant action of body, he charms our attention: sit in a full theatre, and you will think you see so many lines drawn from the circumference of so many ears, whiles the actor is the centre . . . .'

Though Burbage was admired above all others, praise was also heaped upon the apprentice players whose alto voices fitted them for the parts of women. A spectator at Oxford in 1610 records how the audience were reduced to tears by the pathos of Desdemona's death. The puritans who fumed about the biblical prohibition upon cross-dressing and the encouragement to sodomy constituted by the sight of an adult male kissing a teenage boy on stage were a small minority. Little is known, however, about the characteristics of the leading apprentices in Shakespeare's company. It may perhaps be inferred that one was a lot taller than the other, since Shakespeare often wrote for a pair of female friends, one tall and fair, the other short and dark (Helena and Hermia, Rosalind and Celia, Beatrice and Hero).

We know little about Shakespeare's own acting roles – an early allusion indicates that he often took royal parts, and a venerable tradition gives him old Adam in *As You Like It* and the ghost of old King Hamlet. Save for Burbage's lead roles and the generic part of the clown, all such castings are mere speculation. We do not even know for sure whether the original Falstaff was Will Kempe or another actor who specialized in comic roles, Thomas Pope.

Kempe left the company in early 1599. Tradition has it that he fell out with Shakespeare over the matter of excessive improvisation. He was replaced by Robert Armin, who was less of a clown and more of a cerebral wit: this explains the difference between such parts as Lancelet Gobbo and Dogberry, which were written for Kempe, and the more verbally sophisticated Feste and Lear's Fool, which were written for Armin.

One thing that is clear from surviving 'plots' or story-boards of plays from the period is that a degree of doubling was necessary. *2 Henry VI* has over sixty speaking parts, but more than half of the characters only appear in a single scene and most scenes have only six to eight speakers. At a stretch, the play could be performed by thirteen actors. When Thomas Platter saw *Julius Caesar* at the Globe in 1599, he noted that there were about fifteen. Why doesn't Paris go to the Capulet ball in *Romeo and Juliet?* Perhaps because he was doubled with Mercutio, who does. In *The Winter's Tale*, Mamillius might have come back as Perdita and Antigonus been doubled by Camillo, making the partnership with Paulina at the end a very neat touch. Titania and Oberon are often played by the same pair as Hippolyta and Theseus, suggesting a symbolic matching of the rulers of the worlds of night and day, but it is questionable whether there would have been time for the necessary costume changes. As so often, one is left in a realm of tantalizing speculation.

THE KING'S MAN

On Queen Elizabeth's death in 1603, the new king, James I, who had held the Scottish throne as James VI since he had been an infant, immediately took the Lord Chamberlain's Men under his direct patronage. Henceforth they would be the King's Men, and for the rest of Shakespeare's career they were favoured with far more court performances than any of their rivals. There even seem to have been rumours early in the reign that Shakespeare and Burbage were being considered for knighthoods, an unprecedented honour for mere actors – and one that in the event was not accorded to a member of the profession for nearly three hundred years, when the title was bestowed upon Henry Irving, the leading Shakespearean actor of Queen Victoria's reign.

Shakespeare's productivity rate slowed in the Jacobean years, not because of age or some personal trauma, but because there were frequent outbreaks of plague, causing the theatres to be closed for long periods. The King's Men were forced to spend many months on the road. Between November 1603 and 1608, they were to be found at various towns in the south and Midlands, though Shakespeare probably did not tour with them by this time. He had bought a large house back home in Stratford and was accumulating other property. He may indeed have stopped acting soon after the new king took the throne. With the London theatres closed so much of the time and a large repertoire on the stocks, Shakespeare seems to have focused his energies on writing a few long and complex tragedies that could have been played on demand at court: *Othello*, *King Lear*, *Antony and Cleopatra*, *Coriolanus* and *Cymbeline* are among his longest and poetically grandest plays. *Macbeth* only survives in a shorter text, which shows signs of adaptation after Shakespeare's death. The bitterly satirical *Timon of Athens*, apparently a collaboration with Thomas Middleton that may have failed on the stage, also belongs to this period. In comedy, too, he wrote longer and morally darker works than in the Elizabethan period, pushing at the very bounds of the form in *Measure for Measure* and *All's Well that Ends Well*.

From 1608 onwards, when the King's Men began occupying the indoor Blackfriars playhouse (as a winter house, meaning that they only used the outdoor Globe in summer?), Shakespeare turned to a more romantic style. His company had a great success with a revived and altered version of an old pastoral play called *Mucedorus*. It even featured a bear. The younger dramatist John Fletcher, meanwhile, sometimes working in collaboration with Francis Beaumont, was pioneering a new style of tragicomedy, a mix of romance and royalism laced with intrigue and pastoral excursions. Shakespeare experimented with this idiom in *Cymbeline* and it was presumably with his blessing that Fletcher eventually took over as the King's Men's company dramatist. The two writers apparently collaborated on three plays in the years 1612–14: a lost romance called *Cardenio* (based on the love-madness of a character in Cervantes' *Don Quixote*), *Henry VIII* (originally staged with the title 'All is True'), and *The Two Noble Kinsmen*, a dramatization of Chaucer's 'Knight's Tale'. These were written after Shakespeare's two final solo-authored plays, *The Winter's Tale*, a self-consciously old-fashioned work dramatizing the pastoral romance of his old enemy Robert Greene, and *The Tempest*, which at one and the same time drew together multiple theatrical traditions, diverse reading and contemporary interest in the fate of a ship that had been wrecked on the way to the New World.

The collaborations with Fletcher suggest that Shakespeare's career ended with a slow fade rather than the sudden retirement supposed by the nineteenth-century Romantic critics who read Prospero's epilogue to *The Tempest* as Shakespeare's personal farewell to his art. In the last few years of his life Shakespeare certainly spent more of his time in Stratford-upon-Avon, where he became further involved in property dealing and litigation. But his London life also continued. In 1613 he made his first major London property purchase: a freehold house in the Blackfriars district, close to his company's indoor theatre. *The Two Noble Kinsmen* may have been written as late as 1614, and Shakespeare was in London on business a little over a year before he died of an unknown cause at home in Stratford-upon-Avon in 1616, probably on his fifty-second birthday.

About half the sum of his works were published in his lifetime, in texts of variable quality. A few years after his death, his fellow-actors began putting together an authorized edition of his complete *Comedies, Histories and Tragedies*. It appeared in 1623, in large 'Folio' format. This collection of thirty-six plays gave Shakespeare his immortality. In the words of his fellow-dramatist Ben Jonson, who contributed two poems of praise at the start of the Folio, the body of his work made him 'a monument without a tomb':

And art alive still while thy book doth live
And we have wits to read and praise to give...
He was not of an age, but for all time!

SHAKESPEARE'S WORKS:
A Chronology

1589–91	*? Arden of Faversham* (possible part authorship)
1589–92	*The Taming of the Shrew*
1589–92	*? Edward the Third* (possible part authorship)
1591	*The Second Part of Henry the Sixth*, originally called *The First Part of the Contention betwixt the Two Famous Houses of York and Lancaster* (element of co-authorship possible)
1591	*The Third Part of Henry the Sixth*, originally called *The True Tragedy of Richard Duke of York* (element of co-authorship probable)
1591–92	*The Two Gentlemen of Verona*
1591–92 perhaps revised 1594	*The Lamentable Tragedy of Titus Andronicus* (probably co-written with, or revising an earlier version by, George Peele)
1592	*The First Part of Henry the Sixth*, probably with Thomas Nashe and others
1592/94	*King Richard the Third*
1593	*Venus and Adonis* (poem)
1593–94	*The Rape of Lucrece* (poem)
1593–1608	*Sonnets* (154 poems, published 1609 with *A Lover's Complaint*, a poem of disputed authorship)
1592–94/ 1600–03	*Sir Thomas More* (a single scene for a play originally by Anthony Munday, with other revisions by Henry Chettle, Thomas Dekker and Thomas Heywood)
1594	*The Comedy of Errors*
1595	*Love's Labour's Lost*

1595–97	*Love's Labour's Won* (a lost play, unless the original title for another comedy)
1595–96	*A Midsummer Night's Dream*
1595–96	*The Tragedy of Romeo and Juliet*
1595–96	*King Richard the Second*
1595–97	*The Life and Death of King John* (possibly earlier)
1596–97	*The Merchant of Venice*
1596–97	*The First Part of Henry the Fourth*
1597–98	*The Second Part of Henry the Fourth*
1598	*Much Ado about Nothing*
1598–99	*The Passionate Pilgrim* (20 poems, some not by Shakespeare)
1599	*The Life of Henry the Fifth*
1599	'To the Queen' (epilogue for a court performance)
1599	*As You Like It*
1599	*The Tragedy of Julius Caesar*
1600–01	*The Tragedy of Hamlet, Prince of Denmark* (perhaps revising an earlier version)
1600–01	*The Merry Wives of Windsor* (perhaps revising version of 1597–99)
1601	'Let the Bird of Loudest Lay' (poem, known since 1807 as 'The Phoenix and Turtle' (turtle-dove))
1601	*Twelfth Night, or What You Will*
1601–02	*The Tragedy of Troilus and Cressida*
1604	*The Tragedy of Othello, the Moor of Venice*
1604	*Measure for Measure*
1605	*All's Well that Ends Well*
1605	*The Life of Timon of Athens*, with Thomas Middleton
1605–06	*The Tragedy of King Lear*
1605–08	? contribution to *The Four Plays in One* (lost, except for *A Yorkshire Tragedy*, mostly by Thomas Middleton)
1606	*The Tragedy of Macbeth* (surviving text has additional scenes by Thomas Middleton)
1606–07	*The Tragedy of Antony and Cleopatra*
1608	*The Tragedy of Coriolanus*

1608	*Pericles, Prince of Tyre*, with George Wilkins
1610	*The Tragedy of Cymbeline*
1611	*The Winter's Tale*
1611	*The Tempest*
1612–13	*Cardenio*, with John Fletcher (survives only in later adaptation called *Double Falsehood* by Lewis Theobald)
1613	*Henry VIII (All is True)*, with John Fletcher
1613–14	*The Two Noble Kinsmen*, with John Fletcher

FURTHER READING AND VIEWING

CRITICAL APPROACHES

Atkin, Graham, *Twelfth Night: Character Studies* (2008). Detailed account of the characters.

Barber, C. L., *Shakespeare's Festive Comedies* (1959). One of the best critical books on Shakespeare ever written.

Berry, Ralph, *Changing Styles in Shakespeare* (1981). Chapter 6, 'The Season of *Twelfth Night*', pp. 109–19, argues that 1950 was the point when sensibilities changed and it became a less comic, more serious play.

Ford, John R., *Twelfth Night: A Guide to the Play* (2006). Useful chapters on textual history, sources, structure, themes, critical approaches and performance.

Frye, Northrop, *A Natural Perspective: The Development of Shakespearean Comedy and Romance* (1965). A slim work of supreme power.

Hotson, Leslic, *The First Night of Twelfth Night* (1954). Fascinating account, with ingenious detective work and lots of historical details, though the case for the occasion of the first night is not finally proven.

Maslen, R. W., *Shakespeare and Comedy* (2005). Sets the Elizabethan comedies in the context of both theatrical traditions and anti-stage polemic.

Massai, Sonia, ed., *William Shakespeare's Twelfth Night: A Sourcebook* (2007). Thorough account of social context, critical history and performance.

Palmer, D.J., ed., *Shakespeare: Twelfth Night: A Casebook* (1972). Broad collection of early criticism and influential twentieth-century studies.

Potter, Lois, *Twelfth Night: Text and Performance* (1985). Part 1, a useful introduction to the text; Part 2 focuses on productions from 1969 to 1982.

Smith, Bruce R., *William Shakespeare: Twelfth Night: Texts and Contexts* (2001). Detailed account of socio-cultural context.

White, R.S., ed., *Twelfth Night: New Casebooks* (1996). Theoretically-informed selection of essays.

THE PLAY IN PERFORMANCE

Billington, Michael, *Approaches to Twelfth Night*, Directors' Shakespeare (1990). Illuminating accounts by a variety of modern directors.

Brockbank, Philip, ed., *Players of Shakespeare* (1985). Actors' firsthand accounts: chapter 4, Donald Sinden on playing Malvolio, pp. 41–66.

Edmondson, Paul, *Twelfth Night*, Shakespeare Handbooks (2005). Detailed commentary, very good on performance.

Fielding, Emma, *Twelfth Night*, Actors on Shakespeare (2002). Thoughtful, engaging account of playing Viola with the RSC.

Jackson, Russell and Robert Smallwood, eds, *Players of Shakespeare 2* (1988). Zoë Wanamaker as Viola in *Twelfth Night*, pp. 81–92.

Nunn, Trevor, *William Shakespeare's Twelfth Night* (1996). Screenplay of film plus introduction.

Parsons, Keith and Pamela Mason, *Shakespeare in Performance* (1995). Useful introduction by Elizabeth Schafer, lavish illustrations, pp. 227–32.

Pennington, Michael, *Twelfth Night: A User's Guide* (2000). Detailed account, arising from English Shakespeare Company's 1991 production, unpretentious and readable.

Smallwood, Robert, ed., *Players of Shakespeare 5* (2003). Zoë Waites and Matilda Ziegler on playing Viola and Olivia, pp. 60–73.

AVAILABLE ON DVD

Twelfth Night, directed by John Sichel (1969, DVD 2009). Originally produced for television, with Ralph Richardson as Sir Toby, Alec

Guinness as Malvolio, and Tommy Steele as a youthful Feste, with Joan Plowright playing both Viola and Sebastian.

Twelfth Night, The Animated Tales directed by Maria Muat (1995, DVD 2007). Excellent Welsh-Russian collaboration with screenplay adapted by Leon Garfield, voiced by Alec McCowan, Michael Kitchen and Suzanne Burden.

Twelfth Night, directed by John Gorrie for BBC Shakespeare (1980, DVD 2005). One of the best in this series, starring Alec McCowan, Robert Hardy, Robert Lindsay and Felicity Kendall as Viola.

Twelfth Night, directed by Kenneth Branagh (1988, DVD 2004). Based on Renaissance Theatre Company's stage version, starring Richard Briers, Frances Barber and Anton Lesser.

Twelfth Night, directed by Tim Supple (1988, DVD 2005). Starring Parminder Nagra and Chiwetel Ejiofor in a contemporary update, set in multicultural London.

Twelfth Night, directed by Trevor Nunn (1996, DVD 2001). Star-studded cast in a highly intelligent and nuanced reading, including Imogen Stubbs, Toby Stephens and Helena Bonham-Carter.

She's the Man, directed by Andy Fickman (2006). Updated American high-school rom-com starring Amanda Bynes as Viola and Channing Tatum as Duke Orsino.

REFERENCES

1 John Manningham, *The Diary of John Manningham of the Middle Temple, 1602–1603* (1976), p. 48.
2 Leslie Hotson, *The First Night of Twelfth Night* (1954).
3 Leonard Digges' prefatory poem to William Shakespeare, *Poems* (1640), reprinted in 1979 with introduction and notes by Holger M. Klein.
4 Samuel Pepys, *The Diary of Samuel Pepys*, 20 January 1669, ed. Robert Latham and William Matthews, Vol. 9, 1668–69 (1976).
5 John R. Ford, *Twelfth Night: A Guide to the Play* (2006), p. 137.
6 Ford, *Twelfth Night*, p. 139.
7 Charles Lamb, 'On some of the Old Actors', from *Essays of Elia* (1835), p. 149.
8 William Archer, '*Twelfth Night* at the Lyceum', *Macmillan's Magazine*, Vol. L, August 1884, pp. 271–9.
9 Archer, '*Twelfth Night* at the Lyceum'.
10 William Archer, review of *Twelfth Night* in *The Theatrical 'World' of 1894* (1895), pp. 22–31.
11 George Bernard Shaw quoted in *Shakespearean Criticism*, Vol. 26, ed. Michael Magoulias (1995), p. 196.
12 George Odell, *Shakespeare from Betterton to Irving*, Vol. 2 (1921), p. 455.
13 Ford, *Twelfth Night*, p. 143, quoting Elizabeth Story Donno's *New Cambridge Shakespeare* (2004), p. 31.
14 Michael Billington, '*Twelfth Night*: A Stage History', in *Directors' Shakespeare: Approaches to 'Twelfth Night'* by Bill Alexander and others, ed. Michael Billington (1990), pp. ix–xxxi.
15 Billington, '*Twelfth Night*: A Stage History'.
16 Harley Granville-Barker, *Prefaces to Shakespeare* Vol. 6, p. 30.
17 Billington, '*Twelfth Night*: A Stage History'.
18 Grenville Vernon, *The Commonweal*, Vol. 7, 6 December 1940.
19 T. C. Worsley, *New Statesman and Nation*, Vol. XL, No. 1029, 25 November 1950, pp. 498–500.
20 J. C. Trewin, *Illustrated London News*, Vol. 217, No. 5825, 9 December 1950, p. 962.
21 John Gielgud, *An Actor and His Time* (1979), p. 176.
22 Peter Fleming, *Spectator*, Vol. 194, No. 6617, 22 April 1955, p. 502.
23 Billington, '*Twelfth Night*: A Stage History'.
24 Henry Hewes, *Saturday Review*, New York, Vol. XL, No. 29, 20 July 1957, p. 26.
25 Arnold Edinborough, 'Canada's Permanent Elizabethan Theatre', *Shakespeare Quarterly*, Vol. VIII, No. 4, Autumn 1957, pp. 511–14.
26 John Wain, *Observer*, 27 April 1958.
27 Alan Brien, *Spectator*, Vol. 200, No. 6775, 2 May 1958.
28 Peter Jackson, *Plays and Players*, Vol. 5, No. 9, June 1958, p. 13.

29 Robert Speaight, *Shakespeare Quarterly*, Vol. XI, No. 4, Autumn 1960, pp. 449–51.
30 *Shakespearean Criticism*, Vol. 26, p. 199.
31 Billington, '*Twelfth Night*: A Stage History'.
32 Billington, '*Twelfth Night*: A Stage History'.
33 Ford, *Twelfth Night*, p. 155.
34 Ford, *Twelfth Night*, p. 155.
35 Ford, *Twelfth Night*, p. 157.
36 Billington, '*Twelfth Night*: A Stage History'.
37 Kenneth S. Rothwell, *A History of Shakespeare on Screen: A Century of Film and Television* (1999), p. 11.
38 Ford, *Twelfth Night*, p. 160.
39 Ford, *Twelfth Night*, p. 163.
40 Ford, *Twelfth Night*, p. 161.
41 Ford, *Twelfth Night*, p. 161.
42 Ford, *Twelfth Night*, p. 161.
43 Percy Bysshe Shelley, *A Defence of Poetry* (1821).
44 Ralph Berry, *Changing Styles in Shakespeare* (1981).
45 Irving Wardle, London *Times*, 7 August 1970.
46 Hilary Spurling, *Spectator*, 30 August 1969.
47 Anne Barton, *Twelfth Night* RSC programme note, 1969.
48 Berry, *Changing Styles in Shakespeare*.
49 Lois Potter, *Twelfth Night: Text and Performance*, 1985.
50 Sheila Bannock, *Stratford-upon-Avon Herald*, 29 August 1969.
51 Robert Speaight, *Shakespeare Quarterly*, Vol. 20, 1969.
52 Jeremy Kingston, *Punch*, 3 September 1969.
53 Wardle, *The Times*, 7 August 1970.
54 Michael Magoulias, ed., *Shakespearean Criticism*, Vol. 26 (1995).
55 James Fenton, London *Sunday Times*, 24 April 1983.
56 Magoulias, *Shakespearean Criticism*.
57 Nicholas de Jongh, *Evening Standard*, 26 May 1994.
58 Ian Judge, *Twelfth Night* RSC programme note, 1994.
59 James Treadwell, *Spectator*, 6 December 1997.
60 Carole Woddis, *What's On*, 3 December 1997.
61 Janice Wardle, '*Twelfth Night*: "One Face, One Voice, One Habit, and Two Persons!"', in *Talking Shakespeare*, ed. Deborah Cartmell and Michael Scott (2001).
62 Michael Billington, *Guardian*, 27 November 1997.
63 Charles Spencer, *Daily Telegraph*, 27 November 1997.
64 Judi Dench quoted by Wardle, 'Twelfth Night'.
65 Berry, *Changing Styles in Shakespeare*.
66 Bill Alexander, 'A Director's View – A Personal Essay', in *Twelfth Night*, ed. Neil King, Longman Study Texts (1989).
67 Joseph H. Summers, RSC *Twelfth Night* programme, 1969.
68 Alexander in King, 1989.
69 Elizabeth Schafer, 'Twelfth Night' in Parson and Mason (eds.) *Shakespeare in Performance*, 1995.
70 François Laroque, *Cahiers Élisabethains*, No. 32, October 1987.
71 Alexander, 'A Director's View'.
72 Patrick Carnegy, *Spectator*, 14 May 2005.
73 Donald Sinden quoted in '"There is no slander in an allowed fool": Comics, Clowns and Fools', in Judith Cook, *Shakespeare's Players* (1983).

74 Lisa Jardine, *Twelfth Night* RSC programme note, 1994.
75 Jan Kott, *Twelfth Night* RSC programme note, 1994.
76 Magoulias, *Shakespearean Criticism*.
77 Irving Wardle, London *Times*, 23 August 1974.
78 Michael Billington, *Guardian*, 23 August 1974.
79 Bernard Crick, *Times Higher Educational Supplement*, 14 March 1975.
80 Jane Lapotaire quoted in Judith Cook, *Women in Shakespeare* (1980).
81 Potter, *Twelfth Night*.
82 Nicholas de Jongh, *Evening Standard*, 11 May 2001.
83 Patrick Carnegy, *Spectator*, 19 May 2001.
84 Zoe Waites and Matilda Ziegler, 'Viola and Olivia in Twelfth Night', in *Players of Shakespeare 5*, ed. Robert Smallwood (2003).
85 John Caird, interview with Michael Billington, *Director's Shakespeare: Approaches to Twelfth Night* (1990).
86 Terry Hands, interview with Billington, *Approaches to Twelfth Night*.
87 Michael Coveney, *Financial Times*, 6 February 1975.
88 John Caird, interview with Billington, *Approaches to Twelfth Night*.
89 Jan Kott, *Shakespeare Our Contemporary* (1964).
90 Potter, *Twelfth Night*.
91 Elizabeth Schafer, 'Twelfth Night', in *Shakespeare in Performance*, ed. Keith Parsons and Pamela Mason (1995).
92 Carnegy, *Spectator*, 14 May 2005.
93 Nigel Hess, *Twelfth Night* RSC programme note, 1994.
94 Peter Thomson, *Shakespeare Survey*, Vol. 28, 1975.
95 Thomson, *Shakespeare Survey*.
96 Barton, *Twelfth Night* RSC programme note.
97 Wardle, 'Twelfth Night'.
98 W. E. Burghardt Du Bois, *The Souls of Black Folk: Essays and Sketches* (1903), chapter 7.

ACKNOWLEDGEMENTS AND PICTURE CREDITS

Preparation of 'Twelfth Night in Performance' was assisted by a generous grant from the CAPITAL Centre (Creativity and Performance in Teaching and Learning) of the University of Warwick for research in the RSC archive at the Shakespeare Birthplace Trust. The Arts and Humanities Research Council (AHRC) funded a term's research leave that enabled Jonathan Bate to work on 'The Director's Cut'.

Picture research by Michelle Morton. Grateful acknowledgement is made to the Shakespeare Birthplace Trust for assistance with picture research (special thanks to Helen Hargest) and reproduction fees.

Images of RSC productions are supplied by the Shakespeare Centre Library and Archive, Stratford-upon-Avon. This Library, maintained by the Shakespeare Birthplace Trust, holds the most important collection of Shakespeare material in the UK, including the Royal Shakespeare Company's official archive. It is open to the public free of charge.

For more information see www.shakespeare.org.uk.

1. London Savoy Theatre, directed by Harley Granville-Barker (1912) Reproduced by permission of the Shakespeare Birthplace Trust
2. Directed by Bill Alexander (1987) Joe Cocks Studio Collection © Shakespeare Birthplace Trust
3. Directed by Peter Gill (1974) Joe Cocks Studio Collection © Shakespeare Birthplace Trust
4. Directed by Lindsay Posner (2001) Manuel Harlan © Royal Shakespeare Company

5. Directed by Michael Boyd (2005) Ellie Kurttz © Royal Shakespeare Company
6. Directed by Declan Donnellan (2006) Ellie Kurttz © Royal Shakespeare Company
7. Directed by Sam Mendes (2002) © Donald Cooper/ photostage.co.uk
8. Directed by Neil Bartlett (2007) Hugo Glendinning © Royal Shakespeare Company
9. Reconstructed Elizabethan Playhouse © Charcoalblue

FROM THE ROYAL SHAKESPEARE COMPANY AND MACMILLAN

PB: 9780230243804   PB: 9780230243828   PB: 9780230243866   PB: 9780230243842

MORE HIGHLIGHTS IN THE RSC SHAKESPEARE SERIES

PB: 9780230576223   PB: 9780230232105   PB: 9780230232136   PB: 9780230232150   PB: 9780230232082

PB: 9780230576148   PB: 9780230576209   PB: 9780230576162   PB: 9780230576186   PB: 9780230576247

PB: 9780230217850   PB: 9780230217874   PB: 9780230217898   PB: 9780230217911   PB: 9780230221116   PB: 9780230200951

AVAILABLE IN ALL GOOD BOOKSHOPS OR TO ORDER ONLINE VISIT:
www.rscshakespeare.co.uk